Artificial Intelligence: Foundations, Theory, and Algorithms

Series editors
Barry O'Sullivan, Cork, Ireland
Michael Wooldridge, Oxford, United Kingdom

More information about this series at http://www.springer.com/series/13900

Virginia Dignum

Responsible Artificial Intelligence

How to Develop and Use
AI in a Responsible Way

 Springer

Virginia Dignum
Department of Computing Science
Umeå University
Umeå, Sweden

ISSN 2365-3051   ISSN 2365-306X   (electronic)
Artificial Intelligence: Foundations, Theory, and Algorithms
ISBN 978-3-030-30373-0   ISBN 978-3-030-30371-6   (eBook)
https://doi.org/10.1007/978-3-030-30371-6

This Springer imprint is published by the registered company Springer Nature Switzerland AG
The registered company address is: Gewerbestrasse 11, 6330 Cham, Switzerland

Preface

The last few years have seen a huge growth in the capabilities and applications of Artificial Intelligence (AI). Hardly a day goes by without news about technological advances and the societal impact of the use of AI. Not only are there large expectations of AI's potential to help to solve many current problems and to support the well-being of all, but also concerns are growing about the role of AI in increased inequality, job losses and warfare, to mention a few.

As Norbert Wiener said already in 1960, as often quoted by Stuart Russell: "[W]e had better be quite sure that the purpose put into the machine is the purpose which we really desire". But what is this purpose, and who are those addressed by the pronoun 'we'? In my view, we refers to us all: researchers, developers, manufacturers, providers, policymakers, users and all who are directly and indirectly affected by AI systems. We all have different responsibilities, but we all have the right, and the duty, to be involved in the discussion of the purpose we want AI technology to have in our lives, our societies and our planet because AI and its impact are too important to be left to the technocrats alone.

This means that we all need to understand what AI is, what AI is not, what it can do, and most importantly, what we can do to ensure a positive use of AI, in ways that contribute to human and environmental well-being and that are aligned with our values, principles and priorities.

Moreover, we need to ensure that we put in place the social and technical constructs that ensure that responsibility and trust for the systems we develop and use in contexts that change and evolve. Obviously, the AI applications are not responsible, it is the socio-technical system of which the applications are part of that must bear responsibility and ensure trust. Ensuring ethically aligned AI systems requires more than designing systems whose result can be trusted. It is about the way we design them, why we design them, and who is involved in designing them. This is work always in progress. Obviously, errors will be made, disasters will happen. More than assigning blame for these failures, we need to learn from them and try again, try better.

It is not an option to ignore our responsibility. AI systems are artefacts decided upon, designed, implemented and used by people. We, people, are responsible. We are responsible to try again when we fail (and we will fail), to observe and denounce when we see things going wrong (and they will go wrong), we are responsible to be informed and to inform, to rebuild and improve.

This book aims at providing an overview of these issues at undergraduate level and for readers of different backgrounds, not necessarily technical. I hope that you find its contents useful, because there is work to be done to ensure that AI systems are trustworthy and those who develop and use them do so responsibly. And we (people) are the ones who can and must do it. We are all responsible for Responsible AI.

This book would not have been possible without the invaluable discussions I've had with colleagues, friends and participants at the many events where I've spoken. Their questions, ideas and, in many cases, divergent ideas have been a main source of inspiration for my work. It is therefore not possible to list here everybody I would like to thank. However, I would like to say a special thanks to Catholijn Jonker, Jeroen van den Hoven, and all my past and current PhD students and postdocs. I also thank Michael Sardelić Winikoff and Francesca Rossi, for their careful and critical review of this manuscript. Without them this book would not have been possible. Finally, a special thanks to Frank, always.

Virginia Dignum
May 2019

Contents

Chapter 1
Introduction

"As the use and impact of autonomous and intelligent systems (A/IS) become pervasive, we need to establish societal and policy guidelines in order for such systems to remain human-centric, serving humanity's values and ethical principles."

The IEEE Global Initiative on
Ethics of Autonomous and
Intelligent Systems

Where we introduce Responsible Artificial Intelligence and discuss why that is important.

As advances in Artificial Intelligence (AI) occur at a rapid pace, there is a growing need for us to explore and understand what impact these will have on society. Policymakers, opinion leaders, researchers and the general public have many questions. How are biases affecting automated decision-making? How is AI impacting jobs and the global economy? Can, and should, self-driving cars make moral decisions? What should be the ethical, legal and social position of robots?

Many are also worried about the consequences of increasing access by government, corporations and other organisations to data that enables extensive and intrusive predictions concerning citizen behaviour.

The underlying concern in all these questions is: Who or what is responsible for decisions and actions by AI systems? Can a machine be held accountable for its actions? What is our role as we research, design, build, sell, buy and use these systems? Answering these and related questions requires a whole new understanding of socio-technical interactions, the ethical aspects of intelligent systems, and the novel mechanisms for control and autonomy of AI systems.

© Springer Nature Switzerland AG 2019
V. Dignum, *Responsible Artificial Intelligence*, Artificial Intelligence: Foundations, Theory, and Algorithms, https://doi.org/10.1007/978-3-030-30371-6_1

This book is not about the future. It does not present scenarios of doom nor visions of heaven on earth. It also does not focus on super-intelligence, singularity or the other potential areas of AI. Instead, this book is about the present. In particular, it is about responsibility: our responsibility for the systems we create and use, and about how, and whether, we can embed responsibility into these systems. It is also about the accountability and transparency mechanisms that can support taking responsibility.

This book aims to introduce a responsible approach to AI design, development and use. One that is centred on human well-being and that aligns with societal values and ethical principles. AI concerns all of us, and impacts all of us, not only individually but also collectively. We thus need to go further than the analysis of benefits and impacts for individual users, but rather to consider AI systems as part of an increasingly complex socio-technical reality.

Responsible AI is thus about being responsible for the power that AI brings. If we are developing artefacts to act with some autonomy, then *"we had better be quite sure that the purpose put into the machine is the purpose which we really desire"*. (Stuart Russell quoting Norbert Wiener in [103]). The main challenge is to determine what responsibility means, who is responsible, for what, and who decides that. But given that AI systems are artefacts, tools built for a given purpose, responsibility can never lie with the AI system because as an artefact, it cannot be seen as a responsible actor [26]. Even if a system's behaviour cannot always be anticipated by designers or deployers, chains of responsibility are needed that can link the system's behaviour to the responsible actors. It is true that some, notably the European Parliament[1], have argued for some type of legal personhood for AI systems. However, these suggestions are more guided by a science-fiction-like extrapolation of current expectations on AI capabilities than by scientific truth. Moreover, AI systems operate on behalf of or under the mandate of corporations and/or people, both of which already have legal personhood in many countries, which is sufficient to deal with potential legal issues around the actions and decisions of the AI systems they operate. We will discuss this issue later in this book.

For example, where lies the responsibility for a parole decision, for a medical diagnosis or for the refusal of a mortgage application, when these decisions are made by AI systems or based on the results provided by an AI system? Is the developer of the algorithm responsible, the providers of the data, the manufacturers of the sensors used to collect data, the legislator that authorised the use of such applications, or the user who accepted the machine's decision? Answering these questions and distributing responsibility correctly are no simple matters.

A new and more ambitious form of governance of AI systems is a most pressing need. One that ensures and monitors the chain of responsibility across all the actors. This is required to ensure that the advance of AI tech-

---

[1] http://www.europarl.europa.eu/doceo/document/A-8-2017-0005_EN.html?redirect

nology is aligned with societal good and human well-being. To this effect, policymakers need a proper understanding of the capabilities and limits of AI in order to determine how issues of accountability, responsibility and transparency should be regulated.

But what is AI? AI refers to artefacts that perceive the environment and take actions that maximise their chance of success at some goal [104]. The emphasis here is on the 'artificial' as the counterpart to *natural* intelligence, which is the product of biological evolution. Minsky defines AI as *"the science of making machines do things that would require intelligence if done by men"*. Or, according to Castelfranchi paraphrasing Doyle *"AI is the discipline aimed at understanding intelligent beings by constructing intelligent systems"* [44]. Indeed, one important reason to study AI is to help us better understand natural intelligence.

AI represents a concerted effort to understand the complexity of human experience in terms of information processes. It deals not only with how to represent and use complex and incomplete information logically but also with questions of how to see (vision), move (robotics), communicate (natural language, speech) and learn (memory, reasoning, classification).

Although the scientific discipline of Artificial Intelligence has been around since the 1950s, AI has only recently become a household term. However, in its current use, AI generally refers to the computational capability of interpreting huge amounts of information in order to make a decision, and is less concerned with understanding human intelligence, or the representation of knowledge and reasoning.

Within the AI discipline, Machine Learning is the broad field of science that deals with algorithms that allow a program to 'learn' based on data collected from previous experiences. Programmers do not need to write the code that dictates what actions or predictions the program will make based on a situation, but instead, the system takes appropriate action based on patterns and similarities it recognises from previous experiences.

AI systems use algorithms to reach their objectives, but AI is more than the algorithms it uses. An algorithm is nothing more than a set of instructions, such as computer code, that carries out some commands. As such, there is nothing mysterious about algorithms. The recipe you use to bake an apple pie is an algorithm: it gives you the instructions you need to achieve a result based on a bunch of inputs, in this case the ingredients. The end result of your apple pie is as much dependent on your skills as a baker, on the ingredients you choose, as it is on the algorithm itself. And, more importantly, never by itself will the apple pie recipe transform itself into an actual pie! The same holds for AI algorithms: the outcomes of an AI system are only partly determined by the algorithm. For the rest, it is your choice of data, deployment options and how it is tested and evaluated, amongst many other factors and decisions, that determine the end result.

Responsible AI thus means that besides choosing the proper algorithms, you also need to consider the ingredients (e.g. the data) to use and the composition of the team using it. To bake an apple pie, you have the choice between using organic apples or the cheapest ones on sale. You also can ask a starting cook or a star cook to bake it. The same holds for developing AI systems: which data are you using to train and to feed your algorithm? Does it take into account diversity and specific characteristics of the domain, or is it some set of training data that you downloaded for free from the Internet? And who is building and evaluating the system? A diverse and inclusive team that reflects the spectrum of stakeholders and users? Or the cheapest team you could put together and are you relying on poorly paid testers from Amazon Mechanical Turk to label your data? The choice is yours. The results will reflect those choices.

Responsible AI requires participation. That is, it requires the commitment of all stakeholders and the active inclusion of all of society. Which means that everybody should be able to get proper information about what AI is and what it can mean for them, and also to have access to education about AI and related technologies. It also means that AI researchers and developers must be aware of societal and individual implications of their work and understand how different people use and live with AI technologies across cultures. For this effect, the training of researchers and developers on the societal, ethical and legal impact of AI is essential to ensure the societal and ethical quality of the systems and the developer's awareness of their own responsibility where it concerns the development of AI systems with direct impact on society.

Looking solely at performance, AI seems to provide many advantages over naturally intelligent systems like humans. Compared to people, AI systems can generally make quicker decisions and operate at any time. They don't get tired or distracted and are more accurate than humans in those tasks they are built for. Moreover, software can be copied and does not need to be paid. On the other hand, there are many important advantages of natural intelligence. First, you don't need to go far to find it. There are billions of humans available and we don't need to 'build' them, we just need to educate them. The human brain is a miracle of energy efficiency, capable of managing a variety of skills and executing many different tasks at once, using only a fraction of the energy an artificial neural network uses to execute only one task. People are great at improvising and can handle situations they never encountered before in ways that we can only dream machines will ever do.

AI can help us in many ways: it can perform hard, dangerous or boring work for us; it can help us to save lives and cope with disasters; and it can entertain us and make each day more comfortable. In fact, AI is already changing our daily lives and mostly in ways that improve human health, safety and productivity. In the coming years we can expect a continuous increase of the use of AI systems in domains such as transportation, the service industries, healthcare, education, public safety and security, employment and workplace and entertainment[2].

---

[2] One Hundred Year Study on AI: https://ai100.stanford.edu/

It is easy to feel overwhelmed by these possibilities and the rapid pace of AI advances. Already, thought leaders and newspapers are voicing concerns about the potential risks and problems of AI technology[3]. Killer robots, privacy and security breaches, the impact of AI on labour and social equality[4], super-intelligence and existential risks[5] are ubiquitous in the media, making us wary about AI.

In reality, there are many reasons for optimism. According to the World Health Organisation, 1.35 million people die annually in traffic accidents, more than half of which are caused by human error[6]. Intelligent traffic infrastructures and autonomous vehicles can provide solace here. Even if these will inevitably still cause accidents and deaths, forecasts show they can significantly reduce overall casualties on the road. AI systems are also already being used to provide improved and earlier diagnostics for several types of cancer, to identify potential pandemics, to predict wildlife poaching and so improve ranger assignments, to facilitate communication by improved translation, or to optimise energy distribution.

We are ultimately responsible. As researchers and developers, we must make fundamental human values the basis of our design and implementation decisions. And as users and owners of AI systems, we must uphold a continuous chain of responsibility and trust for the actions and decisions of AI systems as they act in our society. Responsibility rests not only with those who develop, manufacture or deploy AI systems, but also with the governments that legislate about their introduction in different areas, educators, the social organisations providing awareness and critical assessment in their specific fields and all of us specifically to be aware of our rights and duties when interacting with these systems.

The ultimate aim of AI is not about the creation of superhuman machines or other sci-fi scenarios but about developing technology that supports and enhances human well-being in a sustainable environment for all. It is also about understanding and shaping technology as it becomes ever more present and influential in our daily lives. It's not about imitating humans, but providing humans with the tools and techniques to better realise their goals and ensure the well-being of all. From the perspective of its engineering roots, the focus of AI is on building artefacts. But it is more than engineering, it is human-centric and society-grounded. AI is therefore transdisciplinary, requiring not only technological advances but also contributions from the social sciences, law, economics, the cognitive sciences and the humanities.

---

[3] See e.g. http://observer.com/2015/08/stephen-hawking-elon-musk-and-bill-gates-warn-about-artificial-intelligence or http://www.theguardian.com/technology/2015/nov/05/robot-revolution-rise-machines-could-displace-third-of-uk-jobs

[4] http://www.express.co.uk/life-style/science-technology/640744/Jobless-Future-Robots-Artificial-Intelligence-Vivek-Wadhwa

[5] http://edition.cnn.com/2014/09/09/opinion/bostrom-machine-superintelligence/

[6] https://apps.who.int/iris/bitstream/handle/10665/276462/9789241565684-eng.pdf

The topic of Responsible AI is also often referred to as AI Ethics, but in my view these are two different concepts, even if closely related. Ethics is the study of morals and values, while responsibility is the practical application of not only ethical concerns but also legal, economical and cultural ones to decide what benefits society as a whole. So, while with Ethics, it suffices to observe what happens, Responsible AI demands action.

Responsible AI is more than ticking ethical boxes in a report or developing add-on features or switch-off buttons in AI systems. Rather, it is the development of intelligent systems according to fundamental human principles and values. Responsibility is about ensuring that results are beneficial for many instead of a source of revenue for a few.

Regardless of their level of autonomy, social awareness or ability to learn, AI systems are artefacts constructed by people to attain certain goals. That's why theories, methods and algorithms are needed to integrate societal, legal and ethical values at all stages of AI development (analysis, design, construction, deployment and evaluation). These frameworks must deal both with the autonomic reasoning of the machine about issues we consider to have ethical impact and, most importantly, inform design choices. These frameworks must regulate the reaches of AI systems, ensure proper data stewardship and help individuals determine their own involvement

Given that values, ethics and their interpretations are dependent on the socio-cultural context and are often only implicit in deliberation processes, methodologies are needed to elicit the values held by designers and stakeholders and to make these explicit can lead to better understanding of and trust in artificial autonomous systems. It is essential to accommodate value pluralism and understand how to design for efficiency, usability, flexibility, resilience, fairness, justice, dignity, happiness, well-being, safety, security, health, empathy, friendship, solidarity and peace.

A responsibility stance applies ethics to the design of AI in different ways:

Ethics *in* Design refers to the regulatory and engineering *processes* that support the design and evaluation of AI systems as these integrate with or replace traditional social structures. Here the aim is to ensure that AI system development teams are mindful of the potential consequences for individuals and societies, by anticipating the consequences of the design choices, reflecting upon the problem being solved by engaging all stakeholders, verifying and validating the design and taking appropriate action to ensure social, legal and ethical acceptability of the system. This means that we need to realise that the principles of Accountability, Responsibility and Transparency (ART) are at the core of the design of AI systems. Ethics in Design will be further discussed in Chapter 4.

Ethics *by* Design is about the ethics of the *behaviour* of AI systems. Work in this field is concerned with (a) the desiderata on the representation and use of moral values by AI systems, (b) understanding meaning and the specification of suitable constraints on system behaviour and (c) the integration of ethical reasoning capabilities as part of the algorithms that determine the behaviour of artificial autonomous systems. Ethics by Design is the focus of Chapter 5.

Ethics *for* Design(ers) refers to the codes of conduct, the regulatory requirements and the standards and certification processes that ensure the integrity of all actors as they research, design, construct, employ and manage artificially intelligent systems. This is to ensure that they consider the societal impact of their design choices and take the necessary steps to minimize negative impact and dual use of their results. This includes adherence to specific codes of conduct and the definition and use of standards, regulations and certification processes that ensure the integrity of developers, products and services. We will further discuss Ethics for Design in Chapter 6.

An important condition for responsibility is knowledge. Therefore, the first two chapters provide the necessary background to understand AI and the role of Ethics. Chapter 2 presents a short introduction to AI, including what it is now and what it can or might be in the not-too-distant future; Chapter 3 gives an overview of the ethical theories that reflect concerns about the impact of AI. The book then continues with a thorough discussion of the principles and methods that contribute to a responsible design process in Chapter 4, where we look in particular at the principles of accountability, responsibility and transparency. Chapter 5 is about ethical deliberation by an AI system itself, and attempts to answer the questions of whether we *can* build such systems and more importantly, whether we *should* build them. The societal impact of AI is the focus of Chapter 6. Here we discuss how to regulate and how to educate such that users, enterprises and policymakers alike are not only aware of their responsibility but also able to take their responsibility as needed. Although this is not a book about the future, in Chapter 7, we end by looking forward and sketching out a roadmap for responsible AI principles that ensure 'AI for good'. That is, AI systems that are trusted, fair and inclusive, that promote human well-being and contribute to sustainability.

Perhaps the most important message of this book is that responsible AI is not about the characteristics of AI systems, but about our own role. We are responsible for how we build systems, how we use systems and how much we enable these systems to decide and act by themselves. Therefore, the last chapter of the book is about us. It discusses the integrity of researchers and manufacturers as they design, construct, use and manage artificially intelligent systems and the ethical implications of AI systems that integrate socio-cognitive-technological structures.

We are responsible for Responsible AI.

This book can hopefully contribute to our awareness of our important role.

Chapter 2
What Is Artificial Intelligence?

> People worry that computers will get too smart and take over the world, but the real problem is that they're too stupid and they've already taken over the world.

Pedro Domingos

Where we learn about the scientific grounds of AI, and current developments on autonomy, adaptability and interaction.

2.1 Introduction

Defining Artificial Intelligence (AI) is no easy task. The field itself is broad and different approaches have provided differing definitions. The aim of this chapter is not to solve this issue or present a single definition of AI but to help understand what are the different claims, and, in the process, understand what today's state-of-the-art AI systems can do.

One of the simplest definitions of an intelligent system is that of a system that 'processes information in order to do something purposeful'.

Another common definition explains AI as a computational artefact built through human intervention that thinks or acts like humans, or how we expect humans to think or act. This is the definition put forth by McCarthy, Minsky, Rochester and Shannon in the classic 'Proposal for the Dartmouth Summer Research Project on Artificial Intelligence', the founding document that established the field of AI in 1955: *"For the present purpose, the artificial intelligence problem is taken to be that of making a machine behave in ways that would be called intelligent if a human were so behaving."* [87].

The above views are concerned with the results that are achieved by a machine rather than with a strict replication or emulation of human intel-

© Springer Nature Switzerland AG 2019
V. Dignum, *Responsible Artificial Intelligence*, Artificial Intelligence: Foundations, Theory, and Algorithms, https://doi.org/10.1007/978-3-030-30371-6_2

ligence. This approach is best exemplified by the well-known *Turing test*, outlined in Alan Turing's quintessential statement: a machine can be considered 'intelligent' if a person interacting with it cannot tell whether it is human or computer [120].

Both perspectives lead to expectations of human-like intelligence and behaviour. However, the type of intelligence currently built into artefacts is far from human-like. Human intelligence is multifaceted, containing cognitive, emotional and social aspects. In fact, [61] identifies nine distinct types of intelligence – logical-mathematical, linguistic, spatial, musical, kinaesthetic, interpersonal, intrapersonal, naturalist and existential. Intelligence can thus best be seen as existing somewhere along a multidimensional scale, in which cognition is just one of those dimensions.

Researchers are far from fully understanding these issues, let alone implementing them into artefacts. Current AI systems only equal human intelligence in very narrow domains, such as playing chess or Go. Moreover, humans are obviously not the only intelligent beings around, and the attribute 'intelligence' can also be used to describe animals and, some claim, in some cases even plants [119]. Expecting AI systems to exhibit human-like intelligence or even to surpass human intelligence[1] may make us blind to many kinds of useful intelligent systems that have been around for some time [25]. In order to understand the reality of AI systems, it's better to take a less human-centric view of intelligence.

Thus, a more inclusive definition is needed to understand current AI. The dictionary defines intelligence as *"the ability to retain and apply knowledge to manipulate one's environment or context"*[2]. In short: the ability to *do* the right thing at the right moment. Given the above considerations, this book considers AI to be the discipline that studies and develops computational artefacts that exhibit some facet(s) of intelligent behaviour.

Such artefacts are often referred to as (artificial) *agents*. Intelligent agents are those that are capable of flexible action in order to meet their design objectives, where flexibility includes the following properties [137]:

- Reactivity: the ability to perceive their environment, respond to changes that occur in it, and possibly learn how best to adapt to those changes;
- Pro-activeness: the ability to take the initiative in order to fulfil their own goals;
- Sociability: the ability to interact with other agents or humans.

These properties somewhat correspond to the criteria of *adaptability, autonomy* and *interactivity* described in [57] and further detailed in Sections 2.4, 2.3 and 2.5 respectively.

Even though many AI systems currently only exhibit one of these properties, it is their combination that signifies truly intelligent behaviour.

---

[1] We will further discuss the issue of super-intelligence in Chapter 7.

[2] Merriam-Webster Dictionary: `https://www.merriam-webster.com/dictionary`.

In the remainder of this chapter, we will first introduce different perspectives on AI that come from the diverse disciplines on which AI is based. We then discuss current developments in the areas of adaptability, autonomy and interaction.

2.2 The Background of AI

AI is a large scientific field with roots in Computer Science, Philosophy, Mathematics, Psychology, Cognitive Science and many other disciplines. Each of these perspectives describes AI in slightly different ways. As discussed above, Computer Science is concerned with the development of computational systems that exhibit characteristics of intelligence. Philosophy is concerned with the meaning of intelligence and its relation to artificial entities. Psychology helps us understand how people interact with each other and with (intelligent) artefacts. Cognitive Science provides essential insights into human cognition. Many concrete applications of AI require mathematics (e.g. to optimise AI algorithms), electronic components (sensors, microprocessors, etc.), and mechanical actuators (hydraulic, pneumatic, electric, etc.).

From the perspective of Responsible AI, the main issues of concern are how AI systems are developed and the societal implications of intelligent action by such systems. Thus, in the remainder of this section, we focus on understanding AI from the fields of Computer Science and Philosophy.

2.2.1 The Computer Science and Engineering View

In Computer Science, AI is the discipline concerned with building artificial systems that exhibit characteristics we associate with intelligence. From these systems, we can also gain a better understanding of how human intelligence works.

Computing brings together two main perspectives on AI. Firstly, the engineering perspective, which posits that the goal of AI is to solve real-world problems by building systems that exhibit intelligent behaviour. Secondly, the scientific perspective, which has the aim to understand what kind of computational mechanisms are needed for modelling intelligent behaviour.

According to AI's leading textbook, by Russell and Norvig [104], intelligent systems can be classified into

(i) *systems that think like humans*, where the focus is on cognitive modelling; e.g., cognitive architectures and neural networks;
(ii) *systems that act like humans*, with focus on simulating human activity, evaluated by applying Turing-like tests;

(iii) *systems that think rationally*, by using logic-based approaches to model uncertainty and deal with complexity (e.g., problem solvers, inference, theorem provers and optimisation);

(iv) *systems that act rationally*, where the focus is on agents that maximise the expected value of their performance in their environment.

AI can also be classified according to the methods used [43], such as symbolic AI (using logic), connectionistic (inspired by the human brain), evolutionary methods (inspired by Darwinian evolution), probabilistic inference (based on Bayesian networks), and analogical methods (based on extrapolation).

Building intelligent machines has many different facets, including understanding language, solving problems, planning, recognising images and patterns, communicating, learning and many more. Different areas of research are characterised by the means they employ to achieve these aims. This is why sub-fields of AI, such as machine learning, natural language understanding, pattern recognition, evolutionary and genetic computing, expert systems or speech processing, sometimes have very little in common. In fact, AI research and application encompasses many fields and not everybody agrees on how these different sub-fields are related or whether they should be considered to be sub-fields. Figure 2.1 attempts to provide a possible classification of these areas.[3]

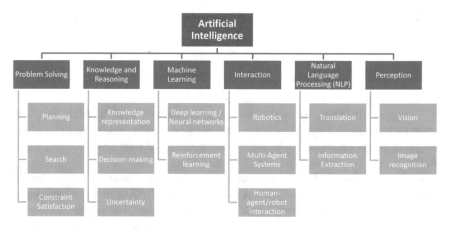

Figure 2.1: Main current streams in AI

Nevertheless, there are two main schools of thought about how we approach AI development. The first aims to explicitly design a system's behaviour from a top-down perspective and the second takes a bottom-up ap-

---

[3] There are obviously other possible classifications and more areas could be included, but the aim of the figure is to provide a general, non-exhaustive overview.

proach, attempting to build intelligence by observation of patterns in the environment.

The *top-down approach* to AI, sometimes also known as *symbolic AI*, or *Good Old-Fashioned AI* (GOFAI), attempts to explicitly represent human knowledge in a declarative form, i.e. as facts and rules. This approach focuses on the translation of often implicit or procedural knowledge into formal knowledge representation rules (often of the type `if-then` clauses) to make deductions, derive new knowledge and inform action. Symbolic AI has had some impressive successes in a variety of fields. The main examples are expert systems, which can approach human expertise but only in very specific problem solving situations. Mathematical theorem provers are also based on symbolic representations, as was e.g. DeepBlue, the chess-playing computer developed by IBM, which was the first computer system that won at chess against a reigning world champion.[4] But this approach has also encountered several challenges that may prove impossible to solve. One example is the common-sense knowledge problem, which refers to the need to explicitly represent the vast amount of implicit knowledge we all share about the world and ourselves. In addition, symbolic approaches have had limited success in areas which rely on procedural, probabilistic, or implicit knowledge such as sensory processes or pattern matching.

Top-down approaches are mostly grounded on the notion that intelligence can be reproduced by rational logic. The advantage of such approaches is the tools offered by mathematical logic to formalise the complex tasks to be accomplished by artificial intelligence machines. However, many mundane tasks are not amenable to be formalised by logical techniques.

Given the inherent uncertainty of many domains, *bottom-up approaches* attempt to model cognitive processes directly from previous experience. This perspective on AI, based on learning from experience, approaches intelligence without explicit representations of knowledge. Sometimes referred to as *sub-symbolic* or *connectionistic* approaches, these systems loosely take inspiration from how the brain works and are generally associated with the metaphor of a neuron, and are indeed the basis for neural network architectures (see more in Section 2.4.2). These approaches require large amounts of data and are particularly well suited to solve domain-specific problems. Their success, therefore, depends on the availability of data and computational power. The use of a shared mathematical language has also permitted a high level of collaboration with more established fields (such as mathematics, economics or operations research). Stuart Russell and Peter Norvig describe this movement as nothing less than a "revolution" [104]. Even though some critics argue that these techniques are too focused on particular problems and have failed to address the long-term goal of general intelligence [81], today it is the power of these approaches that drives the current success in AI.

---

[4] Cf. https://www.ibm.com/ibm/history/ibm100/us/en/icons/deepblue/.

Another driver of AI research is the goal of emulating human cognition on a computer. Here, the objective is to understand how the human brain works and to demonstrate that it is possible to build machines that have all the capabilities of a human (or at least a small animal). This perspective is based on the idea that physical and chemical processes bring about important functions of the mind such as learning, memory and consciousness, and these processes can, in principle, be simulated by a machine. A major proponent of this perspective was Marvin Minsky, who describes AI as mechanisms that emulate the human brain, including the development of specialised hardware. A most notable example is the current EU flagship program, the Human Brain Project[5].

This approach has led to the development of neural networks, which model reasoning as a series of information exchanges between a collection of interconnected units called artificial neurons, similar to the processes in the human brain.

2.2.2 The Philosophy View

The central concepts of Artificial Intelligence (e.g. action, goals, knowledge, belief, consciousness) have long been the focus of philosophical reflection. But where Computer Science mostly takes an engineering stance, concerned with the question of how to *build* these concepts into machines, Philosophy generally takes a more abstract stance, asking what these concepts *mean*. That is, Philosophy strives to answer questions such as: What does it mean for a machine to act intelligently? And what, if anything, are the differences between human intelligence, machine intelligence and other types of intelligence?

Like computer science, philosophy includes many differing views on AI, which have been the basis for the approaches used in computer science. In 1976, Allen Newell and Herbert A. Simon proposed that 'symbol manipulation' is the essence of both human and machine intelligence. These ideas led to the so-called *Symbolic* AI approaches we have presented in the previous subsection. Symbolic AI was intended to produce general, human-like intelligence, through which a machine can perform any intellectual task that a human being can.

Later, Hubert Dreyfus argued that human intelligence and expertise depend primarily on unconscious instincts rather than conscious reasoning, and that these unconscious skills could never be captured in computational rules [45]. Searle extended this line of thinking with his famous 'Chinese Room' experiment, showing that symbolic manipulation, without any knowledge of the meaning of those symbols, is enough to fool an observer on whether an agent is behaving intelligently [110]. Since then, as we've seen in the previ-

---

[5] See https://www.humanbrainproject.eu/.

ous subsection, *sub-symbolic* approaches to AI, such as neural nets, or evolutionary algorithms, based on simulated unconscious reasoning and learning, are currently extremely successful in making predictions that approach the accuracy of human performance in specific domains.

Philosophy also reflects on the question of whether a machine can have a mind, mental states and consciousness. Related questions explore the meaning of machine intelligence, and the relation between intelligence and consciousness. Although most philosophers today say that intelligence does not require consciousness, the question of machine consciousness is central in philosophical studies of AI. One of these views contends that consciousness stems from the structure of the models that intelligent systems use to reason about themselves. But in order to explain how an information-processing system can have a model of something, there must exist a prior notion of intentionality that explains why and how symbols inside the system can refer to things [88]. This symbolic view of consciousness and thought was the leading view in the early days of AI.

Another issue related to consciousness is human dignity, a core principle of the Universal Declaration of Human Rights, which states: *"All human beings are born free and equal in dignity and rights. They are endowed with reason and conscience and should act towards one another in a spirit of brotherhood."* Currently there is growing interest in the effects of intelligent machines on human dignity, in particular considering the healthcare and law domains.

The main question here is whether or not machines are able to fully respect human dignity in their decisions and shows of empathy. If machines replace humans in situations where empathy is a must, then people may become alienated, devalued and frustrated. As early as 1976, Joseph Weizenbaum argued that AI technology should not be used to replace people in positions that require respect and care. On the other hand, other scholars have argued that where it concerns minorities, an 'impartial' machine may be fairer in its decisions than a human [7].

Finally, Philosophy also reflects on the concept of super-intelligence [20], or singularity [80, 130], the hypothesis that AI will evolve into increasingly intelligent systems that will abruptly trigger runaway technological growth, resulting in extreme changes to human civilisation or even its extinction. In his 2011 book Superintelligence, philosopher Nick Bostrom expressed his concern that a super-intelligent machine could one day spontaneously generate goals of self-preservation, which might bring it to compete with humans for resources. [20]. Bostrom's work has illustrated many potential risks and challenges associated with (general) artificial intelligence, but these ideas are not supported by a large group of AI researchers. Critics claim that there is no evidence that cognitive intelligence necessarily leads to self-preservation, and that even if it is logically possible, super-intelligence is utterly unlikely [54]. Others claim that focusing on the risks of super-intelligence may prove a distraction from the many real and valid concerns about AI, from the consequences of its bias, to its impact on jobs, to its uses in autonomous weapons systems. Moreover, predictions that super-intelligence will happen within a foreseeable horizon are not supported by existing data [49]. We will further reflect on the issue of super-intelligence in Chapter 7.

2.2.3 Other Views on AI

In Psychology and Cognitive Science, researchers study how the mind operates, how we behave and how our brains process information. These fields aim to map out and understand cognition, human or otherwise. Here AI is an invaluable tool to explore different theories of cognition, with computer simulations being used to explain existing data and predict new findings.

In Sociology, researchers have proposed two basic approaches to understand human behaviour: *agency*, which refers to the capacity of individuals to act independently and to make their own free choices, and *structure*, which refers to the recurrent patterned arrangements that influence or limit the choices and opportunities available [11].

Even though there is no universally accepted definition, Sociology and Economics see an agent as an entity that acts on behalf of another, without direct intervention from the latter. This view encompasses the common dictionary definitions of agency (see box).

Agency is thus the capacity of individuals to act independently and to make their own choices. Even though Sociology has long debated whether structure or agency are the basis for human behaviour, the principle of agency is leading in most AI research, as primarily exemplified by the seminal textbook by Russell and Norvig [104].

Definition of **agent** (from www. merriam-webster.com):

1. one that acts or exerts power; something that produces or is capable of producing an effect
2. one who is authorised to act for or in the place of another

The concept of agency is also central to Economics, in particular where it concerns the relationship between an agent and its principal. The principal-agent problem occurs when one person or entity (the 'agent') is able to make decisions and/or take actions on behalf of, or that impact, another person or entity: the 'principal'. In AI, it is particularly relevant to understand this dilemma when one of the two participants is an intelligent machine.

In order to ensure that the agent achieves its intended goals, contracts or other forms of agreement are usually drawn up to specify incentives and penalties for the interaction. The agency stance is also useful because it will enable us in later chapters to discuss morality and responsibility in the context of AI systems.

2.2.4 AI Agency

Given the central role of the concept of agency in AI, this chapter will further discuss AI from the perspective of the main characteristics of agency as proposed by Floridi [53]: Autonomy, Adaptability and Interactivity, depicted in Figure 2.2:

- **Autonomy**: the capacity of an agent to act independently and to make its own free choices.
- **Adaptability**: the capability of learning from one's own experiences, sensations and interactions in order to be able to react flexibly to changes in the environment.
- **Interactivity**: the capability of an agent to perceive and interact with other agents, be they human or artificial, understanding that these are agents themselves, with their own goals and capabilities.

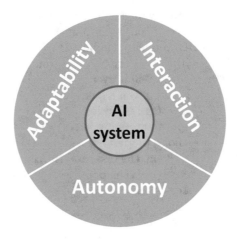

Figure 2.2: AI agency characteristics: Autonomy, Adaptability, Interactivity

In the following sections, we look at these three principles in more detail with a focus on state-of-the-art research.

2.3 Autonomy

Autonomy is perhaps the single most-cited aspect of Artificial Intelligence. It is both seen as a synonym for intelligence, as well as that characteristic of AI that people are most concerned about. It is often the focus of fearmongers and science fiction. The image of a malicious autonomous intelligent machine has always fired up our imaginations. But what is autonomy? And what does it mean for a machine to be autonomous?

The concept of autonomy in AI is usually defined with respect to the environment, e.g. as described in the seminal definition of autonomous agent by Jennings and Wooldridge: *"an agent is a computer system that is situated in some environment and is capable of autonomous action in that environment in order to meet its design objectives."* [74]. That is, autonomy refers to the separation of concerns between the agent and its environment. It also refers to the ability of the agent to control its own internal state and behaviour without explicit external command. However, in human settings, autonomy often refers to the social context, i.e. to autonomy from other agents.

In AI, agents are sometimes described following the Beliefs, Desires and Intentions (BDI) model of human practical reasoning proposed by Bratman [23]. In BDI, beliefs represent knowledge of the world, desires or goals represent some desired end state, and intentions correspond to potential plans the agent has to achieve its desires. Depending on its beliefs about the world, the agent will select a plan that will enable it reach one of its desires. Several computational architectures and computer languages for developing software agents are based on the BDI model, including 2APL [33], and Jason [19].

It is important to note that the term 'autonomous system' is technically somewhat of a misnomer. No system is ever autonomous in all situations and for all tasks. On the other hand, given a sufficiently limited and well-defined context, even a very simple system can perform autonomously [22]. Therefore, in order to grasp the concept of autonomy in AI, we need to understand two issues. Firstly, autonomy is not a property of a system but rather the result of an interaction between the system, the task, and the context, or environment. Secondly, autonomy is not an emergent property, but something that needs to be designed into the system. In Chapter 4, we will focus on why and when we would want to give autonomy to artificial systems. In the remainder of this section, we discuss the concept of *autonomous agent* as it is commonly used in AI, in greater detail.

2.3.1 Autonomous Agents and Multi-agent Systems

Viewing AI systems from the perspective of autonomy provides several advantages. Firstly, it enables us to design and implement systems independently of each other and of their environment; and enables us to coordinate the behaviour of systems composed of multiple agents (i.e. multi-agent systems) as if there is no central planner or controller. Secondly, no impositions are made on the behaviour of the system: each agent can be cooperative, selfish, honest or not. The downside, however, is that the development of multi-agent systems requires explicit efforts to specify how the communication between agents should happen, and how agents can monitor each other's actions.

In this chapter, we take the definition of artificial autonomous agent put forward by Wooldridge and Jennings: an agent is an encapsulated computer system that is situated in some environment and is capable of flexible, responsive and proactive action in that environment in order to meet its goals [137]. Figure 2.3 depicts such an agent situated in an environment where other agents also exist.

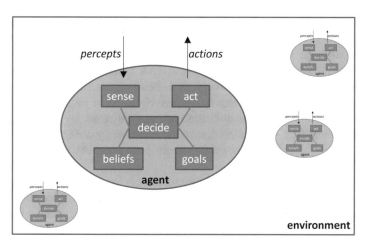

Figure 2.3: An autonomous agent perceives and acts in an environment based on its beliefs and goals

This definition raises some issues worth noting:

- *Situatedness and encapsulation* refer to the assumption that the system under focus is explicitly distinct from its environment. That is, the agent exists in an environment (that possibly includes other agents) but is functionally and structurally different from that environment. Sensors and actuators are needed for the interaction between agent and environment. Agents do not necessarily only act on physical environments, but also in the virtual case the interaction between agent and environment happens through clearly defined interfaces, the virtual sensors and actuators.
- *Reactive and proactive action* refer to the ways the agent decides on an action: either as a reaction to its perception of the environment; or as a means to achieve its goals.

- *Flexibility* refers to the capability of the agent to adapt to its environment by updating its beliefs about the environment. This does not necessarily mean that the agent needs to be able to learn (i.e. be able to modify its own behaviour based on external inputs), but simply that at the least, it should be able perceive changes in the environment and act accordingly.

Note that the above definition of agent does not refer to intelligence. In fact, the agent paradigm applies to many types of systems, not all of which we would consider intelligent. The most often cited example of a non-intelligent agent is a thermostat.

Moreover, the definition also does not refer to the relationships between the different agents in the environment. Nevertheless, the autonomous agent paradigm is mostly applied to distributed problem solving and planning in domains such as online trading and auctions, disaster response and complex scheduling. Multi-agent systems are used to solve problems that are difficult or impossible for an individual agent or a monolithic system to solve. Much research on this topic focuses on the organisational structures (including self-organisation methods and normative systems) and the interaction mechanisms (including game theory and social choice methods) that enable agents to coordinate with others to achieve common or individual objectives.

In order to coexist in an environment, agents must be able to perceive actions of others (e.g. by explicit communication, or by observation of changes in that environment) and to pursue their own goals with, or despite, the activities of others.

Multi-agent systems are also useful paradigms for modelling and analysing social phenomena, typically human societies. To do this, modellers design agents to represent the behaviour of specific individuals or groups, and their interactions in a (more or less) constrained environment to understand the emergence of global behaviour.

Work on agent organisations and agent interaction has provided relevant insights into the incentives, constraints and results of the interactions between different types of agents, without needing to know the inner mechanisms those entities use to realise their behaviours [4]. In a world where AI systems are increasingly complex and opaque, the ability to reason about possible global results, without the requirement to know how the algorithm is designed, provides a potential way to monitor and evaluate AI systems that may prove more suitable than 'opening the black box'.

2.3.2 Levels of Autonomy

The dictionary defines autonomy as: (i) the right or condition of self-government; (ii) freedom from external control or influence; independence. That is, even though the concepts of intelligence and autonomy are often conflated with regard to AI systems, taken strictly, there is nothing in the definition of autonomy that implies intelligence. An agent can be autonomous and dumb, or it can be not autonomous but intelligent.

When considering the autonomy of an artificial system, one defining characteristic is that the system must have the ability to select between options. Thus, the results of autonomous decision-making by AI systems depend on which options are available to the system to choose from. Autonomy can refer either to the tasks or the goals of the agent:

- Task autonomy is the ability of a system to adjust its behaviour, by forming new plans to fulfil a goal, or by choosing between goals. This is for example the case of a navigation system that is able to determine the best route to get to a destination, possibly adapting for traffic and road conditions.
- Goal autonomy is the ability to introduce new goals, modify existing goals, and quit active goals [78]. This would be the case of a navigation system that would determine itself which destination would be the most appropriate to drive its user to.

Task autonomy is relative to the 'means' or instrumental sub-goals accessible to the agent. This is what Castelfranchi refers to as executive autonomy [27]. On the other hand, goal or motivational autonomy refers to the 'ends' of the agent's activity, and the ability of the agent to accept or refuse requests from other agents, and to decide about its own motives.

Moreover, social autonomy is based on the dependencies of agents on each other and their ability to influence each other. Agents will then be able to alter their goals and plans to avoid or exploit the capabilities of others, or to exert their influence on others in order to induce certain behaviour from them. Thus, a socially autonomous agent is one that is able to adopt, or not, the goals of someone else. This may be done for different reasons, including benevolence or selfishness. Whereas task autonomy is usually taken for granted in an AI system expected to act in a dynamic environment, goal autonomy requires a much higher level of trust in the system, and the user needs to be given assurances that these changes of the agent's aims are still acceptable.

In most cases, when someone refers to the autonomy of an AI system, they are referring to its task autonomy. For example, this is the case with the levels of autonomy proposed for autonomous vehicles.[6] This proposal considers six different levels of vehicle automation, from 0 (no automation) to 5 (full automation). However, even level 5 only refers to task autonomy, describing the case in which the vehicle is capable of performing all driving functions under all conditions. Nowhere in this proposal is the possibility of goal autonomy considered: the user still decides where to go.

Finally, autonomy is never an absolute concept but relative to the context: this is known as *attainable autonomy*. This refers to context limitations, such

---

[6] https://www.sae.org/standards/content/j3016_201401/

as constraints on the agent's physical abilities, its reasoning capabilities, and societal limitations such as legal restrictions and social values and practices.

2.4 Adaptability

Adaptability is the ability to adjust something or oneself to change. At the heart of this concept is the idea that systems can perceive their environment. That enables the system to take the most appropriate action and/or to use its perceptions to extrapolate possible future states.

A central issue in adaptability is the capability to learn, which is core to the field of Machine Learning (ML).

2.4.1 How Does Machine Learning Work?

A learning algorithm is a method for learning from data.

These algorithms are often based on stochastic or statistical methods to parse, compare and extrapolate patterns from a set of data. In most cases, these algorithms require data, and lots of it. This data is used to train the algorithms, often over a long period of time, until it is able to correctly identify patterns and apply its knowledge to similar situations.

This approach, *learning from data*, contrasts with the *expert system* approach presented in Section 2.2, in which programmers sit down with human domain experts to understand the criteria used to make decisions, and then translate those rules into software code. An expert system aims to emulate the principles used by human experts, whereas machine learning relies on numerical methods to find a decision procedure that works well in practice.

Classic approaches to AI, like traditional programming more generally, are based on the idea that a hand-crafted model of the domain is necessary in order for the machine to make sense of its input data and produce results (cf. top part of Figure 2.4). These models however, are very difficult to construct, as they require availability of domain expertise, and can be hard to adapt to changing environments. Compared with current ML approaches, they do, nonetheless, provide a much higher level of decision transparency and explanatory capability, which are extremely important issues for a responsible approach to AI, as we will see later in this book.

In order to curtail the difficulties of developing domain models, Machine Learning takes a different approach to system development: in short, instead of developing a model or set of instructions on how to perform a given task, engineers provide the system with (a huge amount of) data about the task and the expected results. The machine is then expected to derive a model from the analysis of all this data (cf. bottom of Figure 2.4). That is, the

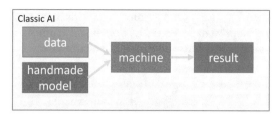

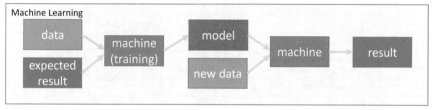

Figure 2.4: The role of models in Machine Learning vs Classical AI

Machine Learning algorithm describes how to 'judge' that data, so that the machine will (hopefully) learn how to perform the task. The resulting model can then be used to analyse new situations.

There are many approaches to Machine Learning, of which the best-known approaches are *Supervised Learning, Unsupervised Learning, Reinforcement Learning* and *Deep Learning*. Even though these techniques differ in terms of goals and approaches, they all aim to give computers the ability to act without being explicitly programmed how to do so.

The goal of Machine Learning is to create a trained model that is able to make generalisations without human intervention. It should be accurate not only for the examples in the training set, but also on future cases that it has never seen before. To apply machine learning, the engineer starts with an existing dataset, which is then divided into a training set and a test set. The engineer then chooses a mathematical structure that characterises a range of possible decision-making rules with adjustable parameters (the algorithm). A common analogy is that the algorithm is a 'box' that applies a rule, and the parameters are the adjustable knobs on the front of the box that control its operation. In practice, an algorithm might have many millions of parameters whose combined result is hard to understand by observation alone. Hence, the use of the expression 'black box' to refer to the opacity of algorithms.

The engineer also defines an objective function, which evaluates the desirability of the outcome of a particular set of parameters. The objective function can reward the model either for closely matching the training set or for using simpler rules, or a combination of these. Training the model is the process of adjusting the parameters to maximise the objective function. This is done automatically by the system, by continuously adjusting its parameters by comparing the actual results to the expected results. Training is the most difficult and resource-consuming step in machine learning. The larger the number of parameters the more combinations are possible, which increases the search space exponentially. Successful training methods have to be clever about how to explore the space of parameters.

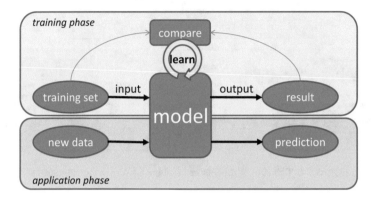

Figure 2.5: Different steps of a machine learning process

Once a system has been trained, the engineer uses the test set to evaluate the accuracy and effectiveness of the resulting model. The model can then be used to make predictions or take decisions based on new data. This process is illustrated in Figure 2.5.

2.4.2 Approaches to Machine Learning

In practice, there are many approaches to machine learning, each with its own requirements in terms of (training) data and applying different mathematical techniques. An overview is given in Figure 2.6 and further described below.

The goal of **supervised learning** is for the machine to learn a function that, given the data sample and the expected outputs, best describes the links between input and output. Formally, given a set of input values x and their results $f(x)$, the aim of supervised learning is to learn function f. This is mostly done by statistical methods, such as *classification* (in the case of discrete functions), *regression* (in the case of continuous functions) or *probability estimation* (in the case of probabilistic functions). Figure 2.7 gives a simple depiction of the classification method, using as example the identification of spam emails based on some features, such as e.g. the presence of common spam topics, poor grammar and spelling, or a sender with email different from that of the organisation it claims to come from.

The main difference between supervised and unsupervised learning is that supervised learning is done using prior knowledge about what the output

Quick Guide to Machine Learning				
Approach		**Unsupervised Learning**	**Supervised Learning**	**Reinforcement Learning**
Objective		Discover structures	Make predictions	Make decisions
Possible Techniques	**Simple domains**	• Clustering	• Regression • Classification	• Markov Decision Processes • Q-Learning
	Complex domains	**Deep Learning** (many-layered neural networks and large datasets)		
Training requirements			Labelled data	Reward function
Example Application		Customer segmentation	Identify spam	Playing a game (e.g. Go)

Figure 2.6: A quick guide to machine learning

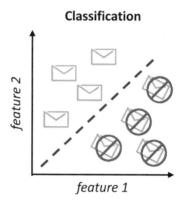

Figure 2.7: Example of supervised learning: classification applied to spam mail identification.

values for the training data sample should be.

Unsupervised learning, on the other hand, does not have any information about the output, so the goal is to identify any structures or patterns present in the input data. The aim of unsupervised learning is to draw inferences from datasets based on the input data without labelled responses. The most common unsupervised learning method is *cluster analysis*, or *k*-clustering, which is used for exploratory data analysis to find hidden patterns or grouping in data. The algorithm will iteratively divide a set of data points (or instances) $x_1, ..., x_n$ into a set of K clusters in which the distance between elements of a cluster is minimised. This method is illustrated in Figure 2.8.

Both supervised and unsupervised techniques are useful to make predictions about the domain, even though these techniques can also be applied

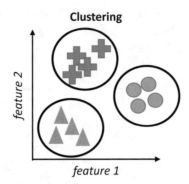

Figure 2.8: Example of unsupervised learning: objects clustered by form and colour

to learn to perform some action in that domain. In these cases, *reinforcement learning* techniques are often the most suitable. Consider the case, for instance, of a robot that moves around in an unknown environment or a machine that is learning to play chess. Given a sequence of examples/states and a reward after completing that sequence, the machine learns which action to take for an individual example/state.

The crux of reinforcement learning is to define the reward function that best helps the agent reach its objectives. For example, if the aim is for a robot to learn how to reach a given position in a room, the reward function could provide incentives for each step that brings it closer to the goal, and penalise steps that move it away from the goal. Assuming an agent that is able to perform actions $a_1, ..., a_n$ and an environment described by a set of states evolving in discrete time steps, the reward function r will associate each combination (a_i, s_t, s_{t+1}) with a reward r_{t+1}. The expression (a_i, s_t, s_{t+1}) means that by taking action a_i at time t in state s_t the agent will be in state s_{t+1} at time $t + 1$[7]. This process is depicted in Figure 2.9. The aim of reinforcement learning is for the agent to learn the policies that will bring it to its goals with the highest possible reward.

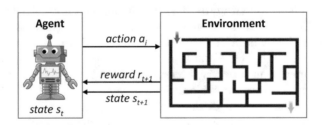

Figure 2.9: Reinforcement learning process exemplified

---

[7] Note that this is extremely simplified; in most cases such a policy is probabilistic.

Deep learning algorithms are approaches to Machine Learning that use Neural Network models and are particularly useful in complex domains. Neural Networks are loosely inspired by the biology of our brains and consist of many simple, linked units (or *neurons*). They are, in essence, attempts to simulate the brain, which is why understanding how the brain works can help us discuss the specifics of artificial neural networks.

In its simplest form, the brain can be described as a large network of neurons (cells that carry electrical impulses). Neurons can pass signals from one to another by synapses of different strengths. The strength of each connection indicates how much one neuron influences those neurons that are connected to it. In neuroscience, these strengths are, in fact, the brain's real information holders. The way neurons respond to the signals they receive is described by a transfer function. For example, a very sensitive neuron may fire with very little input. A neuron may also have a threshold below which it rarely fires and above which it fires vigorously.

In ML, we use the terms that describe these processes in the brain to explain and understand Artificial Neural Networks (ANN), which are also composed of nodes (or neurons) linked by a complex network of connections of different strengths. However, unlike the brain, connections in a neural network are usually uni-directional. An ANN is then organised into input and output nodes connected through a number of in-between layers of nodes, known as the hidden nodes. In an image recognition application, for example, a first layer of units might combine the raw data of the image to recognise simple patterns in the image; a second layer of units might combine the results of the first layer to recognise patterns of patterns; a third layer might combine the results of the second layer; and so on. The structure of an ANN is depicted in Figure 2.10.

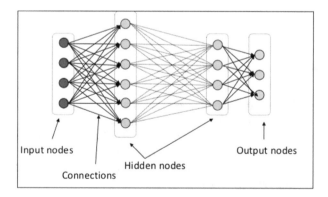

Figure 2.10: An example of an artificial neural network (from [83])

In an ANN, each neuron uses a transfer function to combine a set of input values to produce an output value, which in turn is passed on to other neurons connected to it downstream. Assuming a node y is connected to a set of input nodes $x_1, ..., x_n$ by connections with weights $w_1, ..., w_n$, then the output of node y is a function of these inputs $f(w_1.x_1, ..., w_n.x_n)$. This is the information that node y will pass to its following nodes, with a certain probability determined by its threshold. Learning takes place by a process called back-propagation, in which the end layer repeatedly requests each previous layer to adapt its weights until the result approaches the expected value.

Deep learning is a special type of ANN. Deep learning networks typically use thousands of layers, and often use a very large number of nodes at each layer, to enable the recognition of extremely complex, precise patterns in data.

Even though neural network models have been around since the early ages of AI, they've become relevant only recently when researchers introduced novel approaches to train the neural networks. In 2006, and more or less in parallel, LeCun, Bengio and Hinton successfully developed working approaches [83]. These included a new type of optimiser (stochastic gradient descent); using unsupervised data to pre-train models to automate feature extraction; and making improvements to the neural networks themselves (transfer functions and initialisation).

Each of these approaches was made possible by the growing availability of both the computational power and the data required to represent and train neural networks capable of dealing with realistic situations. The dramatic success of these very large networks at many machine learning tasks has surprised some experts and ushered a wave of enthusiasm for machine learning among AI researchers and practitioners. A well-known early success of deep learning is the work of Andrew Ng and colleagues [82], who were able to make huge neural networks and train them with huge amounts of data (in this case it was to train a network to identify images of cats from 10 million YouTube videos).

2.4.3 Issues in Machine Learning

Because of machine learning's success at solving particular tasks, it can be tempting to extrapolate and imagine machines with a broader and deeper range of capabilities. Many people seem to overlook the huge gap between narrow, task-oriented performance and the type of general intelligence that people exhibit, jumping from machine learning to general artificial intelligence. This extrapolation, however, is incorrect.

Firstly, even within a single domain, machine learning is not a crystal ball. The learning is always based on the available data, and data-based approaches can only predict the future if that future is, in some way, contained in the present. Also, even though many models can achieve better-than-human performance on narrow tasks such as image labelling, even the best models can fail in unpredictable ways. For example, it is possible to manipulate images so that they are falsely labelled by even a well-trained model, although they would never fool a human. Moreover, and most importantly, the learned model is only as good as the data it is trained with. When this data contains bias or erroneous values, or when it is not properly obtained in ways that ensure privacy and are based on consent, the algorithm has no way to know this. It simply identifies patterns it observes in the data, leading possibly to prejudiced or wrong conclusions.

Another challenge with machine learning is that it is typically not possible to extract or generate a straightforward explanation for why a particular result is achieved. Because trained models have a very large number of adjustable parameters, often the training process yields a model that 'works' (i.e. it matches the available data), but is not necessarily the simplest model. That means that even if the decision procedure is known with mathematical precision, there may be simply too much information to interpret clearly. This is the so-called 'black-box' effect. Moreover, the available data has been collected for a given purpose, based on some set of expectations, which means it contains the statistical setup, preferences or bias of those who collected it. Failure to recognise this context dependency can lead to potential bias in the recommendations provided by the algorithms. It is therefore important not only to understand how machine learning works, but also to ensure transparency of processes and decision-making approaches, as well as proper governance of data. We will further discuss these issues in Section 4.3.3.

Moreover, the current popularity of Machine Learning and AI has meant that the terms are often overused. Listening to the media and to the promises of many businesses might lead someone to (wrongly) believe that Machine Learning is everywhere and that every algorithm is a Machine Learning one. However, current successes occur in fairly narrow domains of application. We are still far from being able to generalise over these domains, even to fairly similar ones. For example, once an algorithm has successfully learned how to play Go, or to identify cats in pictures, training will need to start from scratch when we want to apply the algorithm to play checkers, or to identify dogs.

Another common misconception is to equate Artificial Intelligence with Data Analytics. Indeed, both involve the application of various statistical algorithms to derive insights, and so to support decision-making. As a result, the terms are sometimes used as synonyms, especially in business applications, where vendors, developers and consultants are passing Data Analytics solutions off as AI. Gartner, for instance, follows this trend defining AI as a technology able to classify and predict faster and at higher volumes than humans can accomplish without AI.[8] However, AI and Data Analytics aren't the same, and the main difference between them is what is done with the results. Data Analytics is a practical application of statistical methods to large

---

[8]   https://www.gartner.com/smarterwithgartner/use-artificial-intelligence-where-it-matters/

datasets with the aim of providing insights about that data, which are to be used by people making the decisions. Machine Learning, on the other hand, aims at enabling machines to act directly (and in many cases autonomously) on those insights.

2.5 Interaction

A main concern of AI is the creation of machines that meaningfully interact with people and with other machines. By combining human and machine intelligence, we can make meaningful decisions and take meaningful actions in ways neither humans nor machines could on their own. That is, interaction can lead to new forms of reasoning that optimise decision-making and enhance creativity, amplifying both human and machine intelligence through a combination of their complementary strengths.

Whether interactions are accidental, repeated, regular, or regulated, each party will be affected by the interaction. This means that the parties will dynamically modify their actions in reaction to the actions of their partners. Moreover, interaction often strives for collaboration, which assumes that participants are limited in their own resources and capabilities, and therefore each needs others who have resources and capabilities that can extend their own. That is, participants are better off together than alone.

In the early days of AI, much focus was put into autonomy in order to build systems that could replace people in specific tasks. In these cases, there is no need for interaction; AI systems would work *instead of* a person, rather than *in collaboration with* a person: replacement instead of augmentation.

Nowadays, the focus is on the co-existence of AI systems and people, with intelligent artefacts working alongside people in various situations. In interactions between AI systems and people, each brings to the table a different set of skills and capabilities that can greatly enhance the results of collaboration. The study of which qualities humans and machines can bring to the interactions is older than AI itself. As early as 1951, Fitts attempted to systematically characterise the general strengths and weaknesses of humans and machines, in what is known as the HABA-MABA framework ('humans are better at - machines are better at')[52].

An artefact may be embodied (e.g. a robot) or virtual (e.g. a chatbot or a decision-support system) but it should be perceived as behaving like a teammate. This kind of artefact is known as a **cobot**. In these situations, interaction capabilities become at least as important as autonomy. And, as cobots become more proficient at their tasks, it is important that they become better at interacting with others, too. In fact, imagine how troublesome it would be for *"a group of individuals engaged in dynamic, fast-paced, real-world collaboration, to have a colleague who is perfectly able to perform tasks* *alone but lacks the skills required to coordinate his or her activities with those of others"* [22].

AI systems should thus be designed for interaction.

The ability of AI systems to interact with us in a natural way is critical to ensure that they can engage and relate to people in ways that enhance our experiences and support our overall satisfaction and well-being. This requires that they use natural interaction media, such as natural language and non-verbal communication, and that their designers have a sound understanding of what type of relationship people want and need to have with AI systems. In this area, one important topic of research concerns the development of the so-called *human-like AI*, i.e. robots and virtual characters that look and act like humans. This is currently the object of many heated discussions, and will be further developed in Section 4.3.2.

2.5.1 Human-Machine Interaction

With respect to interaction, AI systems can be divided into two main categories:

- **Virtual Agents**, i.e. software systems existing with no direct representation in the physical world. Interaction takes place via computer interfaces. Examples include personal assistants (which may make use of multi-modal interfaces, sophisticated natural-language, query processing and advanced visualisation techniques); intelligent systems, which assist in monitoring, analysing and making sense of complex, uncertain, high-tempo events for example in cybersecurity or disaster management; networked multi-agent systems (that help address data-to-decision problems in for example sensor integration or logistics planning); and avatars or characters in interactive games and simulations. Increasingly invisible interfaces, such as sensor networks or hand-drawn gestures, are being used for interactions between people and virtual systems.
- **Embodied systems**, i.e. artefacts embedding AI technology with a physical presence in the world, containing sensors and effectors, and possibly capable of physical mobility. Examples are robots, autonomous vehicles, smart household appliances and specialised hardware for industrial, commercial, military, space or security applications. Robots are the ubiquitous example of such systems, but rather than the sci-fi image of a humanoid artefact, their most useful applications range from search-and-rescue activities in dangerous environments (e.g. nuclear plants, battle zones packed with improvised explosive devices, or contaminated areas), to medical and surgical tools, companion robots for physically or cognitively challenged people, or simple robotic vacuum cleaners.

Although humans create machines to make their lives easier, they are getting to increasingly depend on those machines for their day-to-day activities, as for example, route planning and location finding, calendar assistance, or searching for information. It is therefore imperative to understand the synergy of this collaboration, and the potential conflicts that can arise. Interaction is more than function allocation or the transfer of responsibilities from one actor to the other; it requires trust and acceptance of each other's limitations. It also requires that the machine is able to explain its decision, an issue we will discuss further in Section 4.3.1.

2.5.2 Affective Computing

Providing information and emotional support are important aspects of social interaction that are studied in the field of Affective Computing [99]. Recent developments in affective computing and social robotics show that virtual agents and robots are increasingly capable of social and emotional dialogues, such as for example the interactive toy of Adam et al., which uses emotional strategies to engage children in a conversation [2] and a multi-modal Embodied Conversational Agent (ECA) that is capable of persuasive affective dialogue [28].

Because there isn't a single unifying theory for modelling emotions, numerous computational models have emerged within the affective computing community. However, the rise of language assistants integrated in our smart phones and homes (e.g. Alexa, Siri, Google Home and others) will lead to the development of systems that will soon be able to understand and react to users' emotions. Thus, we can expect emotional agent architectures to become increasingly available outside of research labs.

Emotions are essential in social interactions because they provide a mechanism for dealing with the overwhelming complexity of social interactions and our physical environment. However, using emotions during interactions with computer systems is not uncontroversial. On one side, emotions are often seen as fundamentally human: the very characteristics that distinguish us from machines. Moreover, Picard argues that *"(j)ust because every living intelligent system we know of has emotion does not mean that intelligence requires emotion"* [99]. In other words, AI systems do not necessarily need to recognise, use or display emotion in order to be effective. However, many others claim that intelligence is strongly grounded in social interactions and the emotions these interactions evoke, so it cannot be disconnected from its socio-emotional bases. According to this theory, known as the 'Machiavellian intelligence' hypothesis, intense social competition was (and still is) the main reason why the human brain evolved into the highly complex system that it is [62].

According to appraisal theory, the most popular approach to modelling emotions, a given emotional state will emerge from an individual's evaluation of her surroundings, situation or contextual cues. As these emotions and their intensity unfold, the individual will likely manifest certain physical and cognitive behaviours. These behaviours could, in turn, further alter the individual's surroundings, leading to further evaluation of the situation, also known as re-appraisal. Over time, re-appraisal serves as a feedback loop to enable the individual to experience different emotional states. Computer models of appraisal theory are often composed of several interconnected modules designed to use emotions and personality characteristics to influence the agent's plans and behaviour [38].

The relation between AI and emotion raises many ethical questions. Emotions are ultimately personal and private. Developing systems that are able to identify, display or otherwise use emotions is seen by many as unethical. We will discuss this issue further in Section 4.3.2, where we discuss responsibility issues related to human-like AI.

2.6 Concluding Remarks

In order to understand the impact of AI on society, and be able to access how to design, deploy and use AI in a responsible manner, it is important to know what AI is. In this chapter, we looked at different interpretations and areas of AI research, and the current state-of-the-art of AI systems, discussing both implications and limitations of these approaches.

2.7 Further Reading

Any textbook on AI would provide useful further reading on this topic. I recommend the classic AI textbook by Russell and Norvig, which is used in higher education courses worldwide:

- RUSSELL, S., AND NORVIG, P. *Artificial Intelligence: A Modern Approach*, 3rd ed. Pearson Education, 2009

On the philosophical aspects of AI, I recommend the reflections of John McCarthy, one of the fathers of AI, available at http://jmc.stanford.edu/articles/aiphil2.html.

For further, and more in-depth, reading on specific aspects discussed in this chapter, I recommend the following:

- On Autonomous Agents: WOOLDRIDGE, M. *An Introduction to Multiagent Systems*. John Wiley & Sons, 2009

- On Machine Learning: MICHALSKI, R. S., CARBONELL, J. G., AND MITCHELL, T. M. *Machine Learning: An Artificial Intelligence Approach.* Springer Science & Business Media, 1983
- On Human-Agent/Robot Interaction: GOODRICH, M. A., AND SCHULTZ, A. C. Human-robot interaction: a survey. *Foundations and Trends in Human-Computer Interaction* **1**, 3 (2007), 203–275; and RUTTKAY, Z., AND PELACHAUD, C., Eds. *From Brows to Trust: Evaluating Embodied Conversational Agents.* Springer Science & Business Media, 2004

Chapter 3
Ethical Decision-Making

"Ethics is knowing the difference
between what you have a right to
do and what is right to do."

Potter Stewart

Where we present the main ethical theories and discuss what it means for an AI system to be able to reason about the ethical grounds and consequences of its decisions and to consider human values in those decisions.

3.1 Introduction

As intelligent machines become increasingly ubiquitous, researchers, policy-makers and the general public alike are growing concerned about the ethical implications. A large part of these concerns relate to the capability, or the lack thereof, of machines to make decisions of an ethical nature. In this chapter, we discuss the design of machines that are able to take human values and ethical principles into account in their decision-making processes. This requires that we first understand the theories that describe how ethics are used to make decisions. The chapter therefore includes a short introduction to the main theories in Philosophical Ethics in Section 3.2.

Determining what is 'good' means that one needs to know what are the underlying values. Each person and socio-cultural environment prioritises and interprets moral and societal values differently. Therefore, in addition to understanding how moral decisions are made according to a given ethical theory, we must consider the cultural and individual values of the people and societies involved. We will discuss this in Section 3.3.

Ethical questions concern judgements of right and wrong, good and bad, as well as matters of justice, fairness, virtue and social responsibility. We therefore define here ethical reasoning as the ability to identify, assess, and

© Springer Nature Switzerland AG 2019

V. Dignum, *Responsible Artificial Intelligence*, Artificial Intelligence: Foundations, Theory, and Algorithms, https://doi.org/10.1007/978-3-030-30371-6_3

develop ethical arguments from a variety of positions. Most people are able to act in ways that enhance or decrease the quality of their lives or the lives of others, and generally know the difference between helping and harming. However, when facing certain dilemmas or decisions, each person draws on their own standards based on their personal values, which results in people making different decisions in similar situations. Commonly, ethical differences are the result of differing individual interpretations of the situation at hand, and may be cultural, political or religious in nature. In the philosophical field of Ethics, various theories have been proposed that attempt to explain these differences and describe what should be understood as ethical behaviour.

This chapter focuses on the ability of AI systems to make ethical decisions, or put in a more precise way, decisions that would have ethical impact if made by a human. This raises the issue of the ethical capability of artefacts. Because of their increased intelligence, autonomy and interaction capabilities, AI systems are increasingly perceived and expected to behave as moral agents. That is, during interaction, users expect the same duties and responsibilities from AI systems that they do from human teammates [95]. These expectations raise issues of responsibility and liability as well as the potential for AI to act according to human values and respect human rights.

Finally, whatever their architectures and specifications, AI systems are built based on given computational principles. As we have seen in Chapter 2, these architectures can vary. However, expecting machines to behave ethically implies the need to consider the computational constructs that enable ethical reasoning, and the desirability of implementing these. Towards this aim, Section 3.4 provides a hands-on introduction to ethical reasoning that shows how results can vary depending on the ethical theory considered. Then in Section 3.5 we sketch a possible reasoning process to handle a perceived ethical situation.

Current discussions of ethical theories with respect to the actions of AI have led governments and other organisations to propose solutions to the ethical challenges. We will discuss this issue further in Chapter 6.

Even though AI offers tools that allow us to better understand the capabilities of moral agency, endowing artificial systems with ethical reasoning capabilities raises issues about responsibility and blameworthiness, which we discuss in Chapter 4.

Determining responsibility in the case of an accident due to system error, design flaws or improper operation is becoming one of the main concerns of AI research. This is of special importance considering that intelligent machines increasingly moderate human social infrastructure (e.g. energy grids, mass-transit systems). Using systems of ethics to account for decisions and actions by artificial systems raises questions with deep implications for our understanding of these systems.

3.2 Ethical Theories

The study of Ethics (also known as Moral Philosophy) is concerned with questions of how people ought to act, and what it means to have a 'good' life (that is, a life that's worth living – one that is satisfying or happy). Philosophers today usually divide ethical theories into three general subject areas: *Meta-ethics*, *Applied Ethics*, and *Normative Ethics*. Meta-ethics investigates the origins and meaning of ethical principles. That is, it aims to understand the meaning, role and origin of ethics, the role of reason in ethical judgments, and universal human values.

Applying ethics to the practical application of moral considerations involves examining specific controversial issues, such as euthanasia, animal rights, environmental concerns or nuclear war. The behaviour of intelligent artificial systems and robotics are also an increasing focus of practical ethics [129].

Normative ethics tries to establish how things should or ought to be, by exploring how we value things and determine right from wrong. It attempts to develop a set of rules that govern human conduct. Normative ethics is particularly relevant to understanding and applying ethical principles to the design of artificial systems.

There are several schools of thought within normative ethics. We focus on three of particular importance to artificial moral reasoning: consequentialism, deontology and virtue ethics. The aim is not to provide a full account of normative ethics, but to show the main differences and similarities between these schools of thought, and how they can potentially determine different behaviours.[1]

Consequentialism (or Teleological Ethics) argues that the morality of an action is contingent on the action's outcome or result. In its simplest form, Consequentialism specifies that when faced with a choice between several possible actions, the morally right action is the one with the best overall consequences. Thus, it follows that actions are equally morally acceptable if they lead to the same consequences. Consequentialist theories reflect on questions such as "what sort of consequences count as good consequences?", "who is the primary beneficiary of moral action?", and "how and by whom are consequences judged?" There are various versions of Consequentialism, including the well-known Utilitarianism of John Stuart Mill [91] and Jeremy Bentham [106]. Utilitarianism states that the best action is the one that maximises utility, where utility is usually defined as the well-being of sentient entities.

Deontology is the normative ethical position that judges the morality of an action based on certain rules. This approach to ethics focuses on whether an action, as opposed to its consequences, is right or wrong. It argues that

---

[1] For more information on Ethics, and in particular on Normative Ethics, we refer to e.g. the Stanford Encyclopedia of Philosophy, `https://plato.stanford.edu`.

Table 3.1: Comparison of Main Ethical Theories

	Consequentialism	Deontology	Virtue Ethics
Description	An action is right if it promotes the best consequences, i.e maximises happiness	An action is right if it is in accordance with a moral rule or principle	An action is right if it is what a virtuous person would do in the circumstances
Central Concern	The results matter, not the actions themselves	Persons must be seen as ends and may never be used as means	Emphasise the character of the agent making the actions
Guiding Value	Good (often seen as maximum happiness)	Right (rationality is doing one's moral duty)	Virtue (leading to the attainment of eudaimonia)
Practical Reasoning	The best for most (means-ends reasoning)	Follow the rule (rational reasoning)	Practice human qualities (social practice)
Deliberation Focus	Consequences (What is outcome of action?)	Action (Is action compatible with some imperative?)	Motives (Is action motivated by virtue?)

decisions should be made considering one's duties and the rights of others. Deontology theories are sometimes called *Duty theories* given that they base morality on specific, foundational principles of obligation. Deontologic systems can be seen as a top-down approach to morality since they prescribe a set of rules to follow. One example is Kant's Categorical Imperative [35], which roots morality in the rational capacities of people and asserts certain inviolable moral laws. The categorical imperative says that one should act according to the maxim that he or she would wish all other rational people to follow, as if it were a universal law. Kant further argues that to behave morally, people must act according to duty. An action, thus, is right or wrong based on the motives of the person who carries it out and not its consequences.

Virtue Ethics focuses on the inherent character of a person rather than on the nature or consequences of specific actions he or she performs. Virtue ethics stresses the importance of developing good habits of character, such as benevolence. This theory identifies virtues, provides practical wisdom for resolving conflicts between virtues, and claims that a lifetime of practising these virtues leads to happiness and the good life. Aristotle saw virtues as constituents of *eudaimonia* (commonly translated from the Greek as happiness or welfare) and emphasised the importance of developing virtues precisely because they contribute to it. He said that virtues are good habits that regulate our emotions, and specified eleven of them, arguing that most virtues fall in the middle of more extreme character traits. Later (Christian) medieval theologians supplemented Aristotles's lists of virtues with three Christian ones.

It should be clear from the short descriptions above that different ethical theories will result in different justifications for a decision. For example, suppose that someone needs help. A utilitarian would look at how helping would maximise well-being; a deontologist would point out that to help is to act in accordance with a moral rule such as 'do unto others as you would have done unto you'; and a virtue ethicist would argue that helping the person would be charitable or benevolent. Table 3.1 compares these theories.

There are many other views on Normative Ethics, such as the *Principle of Double Effect* (DDE), the *Principle of Lesser Evils* and *Human Rights Ethics*, that can be seen as alternatives or extensions to the main theories described above. DDE states that deliberately inflicting harm is wrong, even if it leads to good. However, inflicting harm might be acceptable if it is not deliberate, that is, if it is simply a consequence of doing good. DDE focuses primarily on the intention, rather than on the act or on its consequences. According to DDE it is harder to justify an act that has a bad effect if that effect is intended than if it is not intended.

Human Rights Ethics is another deontological approach that holds that humans have absolute, natural rights that are inherent in the nature of ethics, and not contingent on human actions or beliefs. According to the human rights or human dignity perceptive, each person has unmeasurable value. Thus, when human lives are involved, we cannot use utilitarian approaches to calculate the 'best for most'. In the trolley problem, for example, it shouldn't matter whether a person is alone or accompanied by many or a few; each life counts as much as all the lives together. For a real example of the application of this view, consider how the German government treated a law that permitted authorities to shoot down a passenger aircraft if it was hijacked by terrorists. The law in question effectively allowed the intentional killing of civilians (the airplane passengers) in order to protect other civilians from harm. This law was deemed unacceptable and in violation of the value of human dignity, which is the most central value in German constitutional law.[2]

Finally, the Principle of Lesser Evils is a version of Consequentialism that takes the view that the only way out of a moral conflict is to violate one of the moral positions and choose the lesser evil. For example, if we believe that lying is a lesser evil than helping a murderer, this approach would suggest we lie. This theory implies that it is possible to, at least partially, order actions and situations according to moral value. The existence of such an order has however been contested by others.

3.3 Values

One of the main challenges of ethical reasoning is to determine which moral values to consider and how to prioritise them in a given circumstance. Values

---

[2]   cf.   http://www.bundesverfassungsgericht.de/entscheidungen/rs20060215_1bvr035705en.html

(such as honesty, beauty, respect, environmental care, self-enhancement) are key drivers in human decision-making [101, 108]. According to Schwartz, basic values refer to desirable goals that motivate action and transcend specific actions and situations. As such, values can be seen as criteria to measure the difference between two situations or compare *alternative* plans.

Values combine two core properties:

- *Genericity:* values are generic and can be instantiated in a wide range of concrete situations. In this way, they can be seen as very abstract goals (e.g. eating well, exercising and avoiding stress all contribute to the abstract goal of having 'health', a value).
- *Comparison:* values allow comparison of different situations with respect to that value (e.g. according to the value 'health', you should choose salad over pizza). In this sense, values become metrics that measure the effects of actions in different dimensions.

This means that values are abstract and context independent, and therefore cannot easily be measured directly, but only through their interpretations or implementations. For example, the value *wealth* can include assets other than money, but can be approximated by the amount of money someone owns. Miceli and Castelfranchi discuss in depth the consequences of this indirect use of values in [89].

To strengthen their decision-making and consider a wider range of decisions, individuals tend to rely on multiple values (e.g. environmental care and wealth). However, values can lead to contradictory preferences. For example, cycling to work through the rain might be good for the environment, but will leave you soaked and looking unprofessional at an important meeting.

In order to handle these contradictions, value systems *internally order* values along two orderings. The first one refers to the relative relation between values. Schwartz [108] depicts basic values in a circle indicating intrinsic opposition between values as opposite position in this circle (see Figure 3.1). Values that are close together on the circle work in the same direction and values on opposite sides drive people in opposite directions. For example, 'achievement' and 'benevolence' are conflicting values. This means that generally trying to do something that is primarily good for one's own benefit (Self-Enhancement) is not necessarily the best for others (Self-Transcendence). For example, making more profit by paying low wages is good for the employer's wealth but bad for the employees. However, opposition of values does not mean that one value excludes another value. It mainly means that they are in general 'pulling' in different directions and a balance must be found. For example, if wages are too high the company might go bankrupt and no one profits at all.

In Schwartz's classification, ten basic values are identified and classified along four dimensions. These dimensions refer to desirable goals that motivate action and transcend specific actions and situations: (i) Openness to change: Self-Direction and Stimulation (ii) Self-enhancement: Hedonism,

Figure 3.1: Schwartz's value model (as depicted in [108])

Achievement and Power (iii) Conservation: Security, Conformity and Tradition (iv) Self-transcendence: Benevolence and Universalism. As such, values serve as criteria to guide the selection or evaluation of actions, taking into account their relative priority.

The second ordering is personal preference. Some values are given a relative *importance* over others. When evaluating a decision with conflicting values, people tend to prefer alternatives that satisfy their most important values (e.g. if for you health is more important than wealth, you will tend to buy healthy food even if it is more expensive than junk food). The importance of a person's values determines how he or she will strike a balance when they conflict. The same holds for cultures. Schwartz has demonstrated that moral values are quite consistent across cultures but cultures prioritise these values differently [107, 73]. These societal values also influence moral decision-making by individuals.

Different value priorities will lead to different decisions. It is therefore important to identify which values a society or group holds, when determining the rules for moral deliberation by AI systems.

3.4 Ethics in Practice

Ethical reasoning is particularly important for moral dilemmas—situations where moral requirements conflict, and neither requirement overrides the other [114]. In the face of a moral dilemma, each choice has its own moral justification, and different people can make very different decisions. From an ethical perspective, there are no optimal solutions to these dilemmas. In fact, different ethical theories will lead to distinct solutions. Understanding of these differences is essential to designing AI systems capable of dealing with such dilemmas.

Given the increasing autonomy of AI systems and their deployment in real-world scenarios, these systems will, sooner or later, encounter dilemmas that demand some level of ethical reasoning. Much attention has been given to the ethical dilemmas self-driving cars may face when deciding between different actions, both with harmful consequences for people [17]. This has been described as a concretisation of the well-known trolley problem [58]. This hypothetical scenario, long used in philosophy and ethics discussions, supposes that a runaway trolley is speeding down a track to which five people are tied and unable to move. An observer controls a lever that can switch tracks before the trolley hits those five people, but on the alternative track, one person is also tied to the tracks and unable to move. The moral dilemma for the observer is: Should I do nothing and allow the trolley to kill the five, or pull the lever and kill one? Applications of this dilemma to the self-driving vehicle scenario usually involve the decision between harming passengers or pedestrians.[3] Figure 3.2a depicts the original scenario [58] and Figure 3.2b the modified version involving autonomous vehicles, introduced in [17].

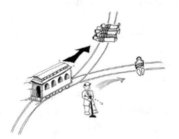
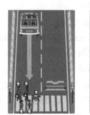

(a) The original *trolley problem*

(b) The Moral Machine dilemma (from [17])

Figure 3.2: Moral dilemmas: trolleys and autonomous vehicles

Trolley scenarios are hypothetical but useful abstractions to consider how we want AI systems to behave in certain situations. Beyond autonomous vehicles, other types of AI systems will also need to confront and resolve moral dilemmas. For example, an intelligent medicine dispenser may need to choose between two patients when it does not have enough medicine; a search-and-rescue robot may need to prioritise attention to some victims over others; or a health-care robot may have to choose between a user's desires and optimal care [31].

---

[3] See http://moralmachine.mit.edu for the most well-known study of moral dilemmas involving autonomous vehicles.

In this section, we analyse how an AI system that's expected to act autonomously can respond to a dilemma given the different ethical theories described in Section 3.2. However, it is important to note that automated solutions to these dilemmas are not the only possibility, and that they are probably not the most suitable or desirable. As we will see in Chapter 4, human-in-the-loop solutions are often the most appropriate for many situations, as they allow for a more clear attribution of responsibilities. However, responsibility does not lie solely with the individual who takes the actual decision, but is the product of societal, legal and physical infrastructures that support or constrain the situation. We will further discuss this issue in Chapter 5.

When considering how to implement moral deliberation mechanisms in AI systems, we must remember that moral dilemmas do not have a single optimal solution; the dilemma arises precisely from the need to choose between two 'bad' options. Of the many ethical decisions that AI systems will need to make, one strong example is the dilemma an autonomous vehicle would face if forced to choose between harming its passengers or harming pedestrians, as introduced above and depicted in Figure 3.2b. This dilemma, however, is really a metaphor used to highlight the ethical challenges that autonomous machines may encounter, rather than aiming at portraying a realistic situation. After all, it's a very unlikely scenario in which either a self-driving car or a human doesn't have the time or skill to avoid an accident and is left with the choice of whom to harm. Moreover, note that the trolley problem assumes (a) reliable and perfect, or good enough, knowledge of the state of the world, (b) perfect control, so the outcome of an action is known, and (c) enough time to deliberate.

Purely as an illustration, we apply the ethical theories described in Section 3.2 to determine the potential reactions of the self-driving car in the situation depicted in Figure 3.2b. The aim is to show that each theory potentially leads to a different decision and justification for that decision, rather than the realism of the solution itself.

- A *Consequentialist*, or Utilitarian, car will focus on the results of its actions and use means-ends reasoning to choose the best outcome for most. It will therefore maximise the number of (human) lives saved.
- A *Deontologic*, or Kantian, car will consider the morality of its possible actions and refrain from choosing an action that it knows would cause harm to people. It will therefore not choose to actively take the action of swerving, if it knows that swerving would cause harm to someone.
- A *Virtuous* car is concerned with its motives and will consider which action a virtuous agent would take. It might then determine that the most virtuous thing to do is to protect the pedestrians as these are the most vulnerable.

It is also important to realise that the decision an individual takes in case of a moral dilemma is also influenced by the way that individual prioritises values. It is easy to see that an agent that prioritises Hedonism will handle situations differently from one that prioritises Universalism.

3.5 Implementing Ethical Reasoning

Many researchers argue that there are many ethical and practical objections to the attempt to implement ethical reasoning in AI systems [79]. These objections include the fact that given that autonomous systems do not experience regret, they are not able to respond appropriately to moral dilemmas; and that these systems lack the creativity necessary to resolve moral dilemmas in different situations. In this section, we consider the overall process of reasoning about the ethical aspects of any given situation, as humans do. It should be clear that this type of reasoning involves capabilities far above what can be currently implemented in AI systems. In Chapter 5 we will discuss in depth whether we ought to implement ethical reasoning into AI systems, and what these computational challenges are.

In order for an agent to apply the type of moral reasoning suggested by ethical theories, it first needs to be able to identify that it is in a situation that has an ethical dimension. This is a complex process and requires not only sophisticated reasoning capabilities but also powerful sensors, actuators and sufficient computational capability to reach a decision in real time. Most of these capabilities are currently out of reach for most AI systems. In short, a possible computational process of evaluating and choosing among alternatives in a manner consistent with ethical principles includes the following steps [115]:

1. *Recognise that there is an event to which to react.*
   Based on the information received through its sensors, the agent must be able to determine that there is a situation that requires action. For instance, a car's sensors might indicate that there is an obstacle in its path. The car then needs to determine how to react to this obstacle. Depending on the quality of the sensors, it will be able to determine size and material, whether it is a person, an animal or an object, and it may even may be possible to determine gender, age, status and all the other factors that are necessary for ethical reasoning as depicted in Figure 3.2b. This level of perception is, however, far from possible with current technology.
2. *Determine that the event has an ethical dimension.*
   The agent will then need to identify the possible ethical dimensions of the situation. For this it will need to determine which parties would be affected by potential responses. For each action the agent could take, it will need to determine the potential positive and negative consequences

as well as their probability and magnitude. This all requires extremely complex reasoning and sufficient data about past situations.

3. *Take personal responsibility for generating an ethical solution to the problem.*
   The agent now needs to decide whether it is its responsibility to resolve the situation at hand, or whether it should alert its user or some other actor about the situation (e.g. police officers or road authorities). We will discuss these issues of 'human-in-the-loop' in Section 5.5.
4. *Identify the relevant principles, rights and justice issues.*
   Once the agent determines that it must act, it needs to figure out what abstract ethical rule(s) might apply to the problem (including any relevant code of ethics). This includes the types of reasoning described above as well as the assessment of the rights of the parties involved and issues of justice and fairness. Here, it is also important to determine whether the decision is influenced by some bias or cognitive barriers.
5. *Decide how these abstract ethical rules actually apply to the problem in order to suggest a concrete solution.*
   Finally the agent needs to generate a course of action, and then
6. *Act.*

The main issue is whether any computer (or human, for that matter) could ever gather and compare all the information necessary for the theories to be applied in real time [6]. This problem seems especially acute for a Consequentialist approach, since the consequences of any action are essentially unbounded in space or time, and therefore we'd need to decide how far the system should go in evaluating possible consequences. This problem remains for Deontologic or Virtues approaches as consistency between duties can typically be assessed only through the analysis of their effects in space and time. Reinforcement learning techniques can be applied as means to analyse the evolution and adaptation of ethical behaviour, but this requires further research.

Different Ethical theories differ in terms of computational complexity of the required deliberation algorithms. To implement Consequentialist agents, reasoning about the consequences of actions is needed, which can be supported by e.g. game theoretic approaches, or by the ability to simulate all possible consequences of an action. For Deontologic agents, higher order reasoning is needed to reason about the actions themselves. That is, the agent must be aware of its own action capabilities and their relations to institutional norms. This type of normative reasoning has been done through formal methods, e.g. employing Deontic logics. Finally, Virtue agents need to reason about their own motives, which lead to actions, which lead to consequences. These are more complex modalities and require e.g. Theory of Mind models to analyse how others (the virtuous examples) would react in the situation on hand, and to deal with the perceived effect of actions on others.

3.6 Concluding Remarks

In this chapter, we have seen how Ethics can be used to guide deliberation in case of moral dilemmas, and considered the possibility of having such deliberation done by AI systems.

Most important is to understand how society will perceive and accept these decisions. In an empirical experiment, Malle found *"differences both in the norms people impose on robots (expecting action over inaction) and the blame people assign to robots (less for acting, and more for failing to act)"* [86]. Moreover, the proposed approaches have different computational issues concerning implementing moral deliberation. However, further research is needed to understand which of the decisions driven by the different approaches are acceptable and useful to users.

3.7 Further Reading

To read more on Ethics, the Stanford Encyclopedia of Philosophy is a very good source of information. See `https://plato.stanford.edu`.

For further reading on specific aspects discussed in this chapter, I recommend the following.
On the Moral Machine Experiment:

- BONNEFON, J.-F., SHARIFF, A., AND RAHWAN, I. The social dilemma of autonomous vehicles. *Science* **352**, 6293 (2016), 1573–1576
- KIM, R., KLEIMAN-WEINER, M., ABELIUK, A., AWAD, E., DSOUZA, S., TENENBAUM, J., AND RAHWAN, I. A Computational Model of Commonsense Moral Decision Making. In *AAAI/ACM Conference on Artificial Intelligence, Ethics and Society (AIES)* (2018), ACM, pp. 197–203

On moral reasoning by autonomous machines:

- WALLACH, W., AND ALLEN, C. *Moral Machines: Teaching Robots Right from Wrong.* Oxford University Press, 2008
- MALLE, B. F. Integrating robot ethics and machine morality: the study and design of moral competence in robots. *Ethics and Information Technology* **8**, 4 (2016), 243–256

Chapter 4
Taking Responsibility

> "How will machines know what we value if we don't know it ourselves?"
>
> John C. Havens

Where we discuss how to ensure that AI systems are developed in a responsible way.

4.1 Introduction

Now that we have discussed what Artificial Intelligence (AI) is and how ethical theories can be relevant to understanding the impact of AI, we turn our attention to the practical development of AI systems in ways that are aligned with human values and can ensure trust.

AI has huge potential to bring accuracy, efficiency, cost savings and speed to a whole range of human activities and to provide entirely new insights into behaviour and cognition. However, the way AI is developed and deployed for a great part determines how AI will impact our lives and societies. For instance, automated classification systems can deliver prejudiced results and therefore raise questions about privacy and bias, and the autonomy of self-driving vehicles raises concerns about safety and responsibility. AI's impact concerns not only the the research and development directions of AI, but also how these systems are introduced into society. There is debate concerning how the use of AI will influence labour, well-being, social interactions, healthcare, income distribution and other areas of social relevance. Dealing with these issues requires that ethical, legal, societal and economical implications are taken into account.

AI will affect everybody. This demands that the development of AI systems ensures inclusion and diversity, that is, truly considers all humankind

V. Dignum, *Responsible Artificial Intelligence*, Artificial Intelligence: Foundations, Theory, and Algorithms, https://doi.org/10.1007/978-3-030-30371-6_4

when determining the purpose of the systems. Therefore, Responsible AI also requires informed participation of all stakeholders, which means that education plays an important role, both to ensure that knowledge of the potential impact of AI is widespread, as well as to make people aware that they can participate in shaping societal development. At the core of AI development should lie the idea of 'AI for Good' and 'AI for All'. We will discuss further this issue in Chapter 7.

Researchers, policymakers, industry and society at large, all are increasingly recognising the need for design and engineering approaches that ensure the safe, beneficial and fair use of AI technologies, that consider the implications of ethically and legally relevant decision-making by machines, and that evaluate the ethical and legal status of AI. These approaches include the methods and tools for system design and implementation, governance and regulatory processes, and consultation and training activities that ensure all are heard and able to participate in the discussion.

In this endeavour, it is important to realise that AI does not stand by itself, but must be understood as part of socio-technical relations. A **responsible approach to AI is needed**. One that not only ensures that systems are developed in a good way, but also that they are developed for a good cause. The focus of this chapter is on understanding what such an approach should look like, who are the responsible parties and how to decide on which systems can and should be developed.

Responsible Artificial Intelligence is concerned with the fact that decisions and actions taken by intelligent autonomous systems have consequences that can be seen as being of an ethical nature. These consequences are real and important, independently of whether the AI system itself is able to reason about ethics or not. As such, Responsible AI provides directions for action and can maybe best be seen as a code of behaviour — for AI systems, but, most importantly, for us.

> **Responsible AI** is more than the ticking of some ethical 'boxes' or the development of some add-on features in AI systems.

In all cases, the processes by which systems are developed entail a long list of decisions by designers, developers and other stakeholders, many of them of an ethical nature. Typically, many different options and decisions are taken during the design process, and in many cases there is not one clear 'right' choice. These decisions cannot just be left to be made by those who engineer the systems, nor to those who manufacture or use them, but require societal awareness and informed discussion. Determining which decisions an AI system can take, and deciding how to develop such systems, are both ethically based decisions that require a responsible approach. Most of all, this means that these choices and decisions must be explicitly reported and open for inspection. This is fundamentally different from but at least as important as the discussion of whether or not AI systems are capable of ethical reasoning, which will be discussed further in Chapter 5.

At all levels and in all domains, businesses and governments are, or will soon be, applying AI solutions to a myriad of products and services. It is fundamental that the general public moves from passively adopting or rejecting technology to being in the forefront of the innovation process, demanding and reflecting on the potential results and reach of AI. The success of AI is therefore no longer a matter of financial profit alone but how it connects directly to human well-being. Putting human well-being at the core of development provides not only a sure recipe for innovation but also both a realistic goal as well as concrete means to measure the impact of AI. We will discuss the issue of education further in Chapter 6.

In this chapter, we first examine how Responsible Research and Innovation (RRI) approaches support the development of technologies and services, and how Responsible AI can learn from such approaches. We then present the grounding principles of Responsible AI, namely Adaptability, Responsibility and Transparency. We then introduce the Design for Values methodology to guide the development of Responsible AI systems. Finally, we discuss how these principles can be integrated into a system development life cycle framework.

4.2 Responsible Research and Innovation

Given the fundamental and profound impact of AI systems in human society, the development of AI technology cannot be done in isolation from its sociotechnical context. A full understanding of societal, ethical and policy impacts requires us to analyse the larger context of its implementation. In this section, we describe how a Responsible Research and Innovation (RRI) vision can be applied to the development of AI systems.

RRI describes a research and innovation process that takes into account effects and potential impacts on the environment and society.

There are many approaches to and views on RRI, some focused on environmental effects and others on societal impact, but fundamentally RRI is grounded on participation. That is, RRI requires that all societal actors (researchers, citizens, policymakers, business, non-governmental organisations, etc.) work together during the whole research and innovation process in order to better align both the process and its outcomes with the values, needs and expectations of society. RRI should be understood as a continuous process that does not stop at the drawing table but continues through the whole process until the introduction of resulting products and services into the market.

4.2.1 Understanding the RRI Process

RRI has been defined as a "transparent, interactive process by which societal actors and innovators become mutually responsive to each other with a view to the (ethical) acceptability, sustainability and societal desirability of the innovation process and its marketable products" [131].

Figure 4.1: The Responsible Research and Innovation process

The RRI process[1] is depicted in Figure 4.1. The process should ensure that all parties participate during the process of defining research and innovation directions. The issue of *Diversity and Inclusion* refers to the need to involve a wide range of stakeholders in the early innovation process, to ensuring diversity and inclusion within system development teams and stakeholders, broadening and diversifying the sources of knowledge, expertise, disciplines and perspectives. *Openness and Transparency* require open, clear communication about the nature of the project, including funding/resources, decision-making processes and governance. Making data and results openly available ensures accountability and enables critical scrutiny, which contribute to build public trust in research and innovation. *Anticipation and Reflexivity* are needed to understand the current context for research and innovation from a diverse range of perspectives. They imply the need to consider the environmental, economic and social impact in the short and long term. They also refer to the need to identify and reflect on individual and institutional values, assump-

---

[1] Adapted from https://ec.europa.eu/programmes/horizon2020/en/h2020-section/responsible-research-innovation

tions, practices and responsibilities. Finally, *Responsiveness and Adaptiveness* are needed to deal with a dynamic context and with possibly emerging knowledge, data, perspectives, views and norms. They require an ongoing interaction with stakeholders and an ability to change patterns of thought and behaviour as well as roles and responsibilities in response to emerging perspectives and insights in the context.

4.2.2 RRI in the Development of AI Systems

Advances in computational autonomy and machine learning are rapidly enabling AI systems to decide and act without direct human control. This means that special attention should be given to the analysis of the evolution of the system, and how to ensure that it does not lead to undesirable effects.

A responsible approach to Artificial Intelligence is needed to ensure the safe, beneficial and fair use of AI technologies, to consider the ethical implications of decision-making by machines, and to define the legal status of AI. The focus of this process should be on ensuring wide societal support for the AI applications being developed, which is achieved by focusing on human values and well-being. Moreover, for the whole of society to truly be able to benefit from all AI developments, education and an honest and accessible AI narrative are needed. Only then, will everybody be able to understand AI's impact and truly benefit from its results. RRI in AI should therefore include steps to ensure proper and wide education of all stakeholders present and future, alongside governance models for responsibility in AI. We will discuss these issues further in Chapter 6.

Ensuring that systems are designed responsibly contributes to our trust in their behaviour, and requires accountability, i.e. being able to explain and justify decisions, and transparency, i.e. being able to understand the ways systems make decisions and the data being used. To this effect, we have proposed the principles of Accountability, Responsibility and Transparency (ART). ART follows a Design for Values approach as outlined in Section 4.4 to ensure that human values and ethical principles, and their priorities and choices are explicitly included in the design processes in a transparent and systematic manner.

True responsibility in AI is not just about how we design these technologies but how we define their success. Even if a system is built to be safe and robust, comply with legal regulations, and be economically viable, it can still have dramatic negative consequences on human and societal well-being. Issues such as mental health, emotions, identity, autonomy, or dignity, which are key components of what makes us human, are not those that are measured by the usual Key Performance Indicators. Multiple metrics are already in use that measure well-being through Indicators such as the United Nations'

Human Development Index[2] and the Genuine Progress Indicator.[3] Business leaders and governments alike have been working for years to implement a Triple Bottom Line[4] mindset honouring societal and environmental issues along with financial concerns. Many are also aligning business with the UN's Sustainable Development Goals.[5] Responsible AI development must thus include the consideration of measuring performance in terms of human and societal well-being.

4.3 The ART of AI: Accountability, Responsibility, Transparency

Following the characterisation of AI given in Chapter 2, in this chapter we assume an intelligent system (or agent) to be a system that is capable of perceiving its environment and deliberating how to act in order to achieve its own goals, assuming that other agents possibly share the same environment. As such, AI systems are characterised by their *autonomy* to decide on how to act, their ability to *adapt*, by learning from the changes effected in the environment, and how they *interact* with other agents in order to coordinate their activities in that environment [57, 104].

These properties enable agents to deal effectively with the kinds of environments in which we live and work: environments that are unpredictable, dynamic in space and time, and where one is often faced by situations one has never encountered before. If AI systems are capable and expected to act in such environments, we need to be able to trust that they will not exhibit undesirable behaviour. Or, at least, we need to limit the effects of unexpected behaviour. Therefore, design methodologies that take these issues into account are essential for trust and the acceptance of AI systems as part of a complex socio-technical environment.

To reflect societal concerns about the impact of AI, and to ensure that AI systems are developed responsibly, and incorporating social and ethical values, these characteristics of autonomy, adaptability and interaction, as discussed in Chapter 2, should be complemented with design principles that ensure trust. In [40] we have proposed to complement autonomy with *responsibility*, interactiveness with *accountability*, and adaptation with *transparency*. These characteristics relate most directly to the technical system. However, the impact and consequences of an AI system reach further than the technical system itself, and as such the system should be seen as a socio-technical system, encompassing the stakeholders and organisations involved.

---

[2] See http://hdr.undp.org/en/content/human-development-index-hdi

[3] See https://en.wikipedia.org/wiki/Genuine_progress_indicator

[4] See https://en.wikipedia.org/wiki/Triple_bottom_line

[5] See https://sustainabledevelopment.un.org/

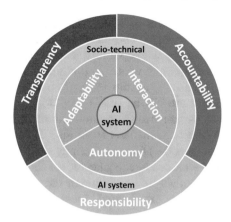

Figure 4.2: The ART principles: Accountability, Responsibility, Autonomy

The ART principles for responsible and trustworthy AI apply then to the AI socio-technical system. That is, addressing ART will require a socio-technical approach to design, deployment and use of systems, interweaving software solutions with governance and regulation. Moreover, even though each of the ART principles can apply to all aspects of AI systems, each is imperative for a specific characteristic, as is depicted in Figure 4.2. That is, truly responsible AI cannot have autonomy without some form of responsibility, interaction without accountability, nor adaptability without transparency. From the perspective of system development, ART requires new methods that support the integration of the ethical and societal impact of AI systems into the engineering process. Above all, ART requires training and awareness of all stakeholders, including researchers, designers, programmers, managers, providers, users, and all of society to enable each of them to understand and assume their role in the overall process.

The ART principles for Responsible AI can be summarised as follows:

- **Accountability** refers to the requirement for the system to be able to explain and justify its decisions to users and other relevant actors. To ensure accountability, decisions should be derivable from, and explained by, the decision-making mechanisms used. It also requires that the moral values and societal norms that inform the purpose of the system as well as their operational interpretations have been elicited in an open way involving all stakeholders.

- **Responsibility** refers to the role of people themselves in their relation to AI systems. As the chain of responsibility grows, means are needed to link the AI systems' decisions to their input data and to the actions of stakeholders involved in the system's decision. Responsibility is not just about making rules to govern intelligent machines; it is about the whole socio-technical system in which the system operates, and which encompasses people, machines and institutions.

- **Transparency** indicates the capability to describe, inspect and reproduce the mechanisms through which AI systems make decisions and learn to adapt to their environment, and the provenance and dynamics of the data that is used and created by the system. Moreover, trust in the system will improve if we can ensure openness of affairs in all that is related to the system. As such, transparency is also about being explicit and open about choices and decisions concerning data sources and development processes and stakeholders. Stakeholders should also be involved in decisions about all models that use human data or affect human beings or can have other morally significant impact.

Given this characterisation, we further define the ART principles in the following sections of this chapter. As a whole, these principles inform the design of AI systems. That is, ART imposes requirements on AI systems' design and architecture that will condition the development process and the systems' architecture.

Note that there is a fundamental difference between accountability and responsibility, even if these terms are often used interchangeably, as synonyms. Putting it simply, accountability refers to the ability to explain, or report on, one's role in events or actions, whereas responsibility is the duty to answer for one's actions. Responsibility entails liability and exists before the task or action is done. Accountability is only evident after the action is done, or not done. When a person delegates some task to an agent, be it artificial or human, the result of that task is still the responsibility of the delegating person (principal), who is the one who will be liable if things don't go as expected. The agent however, must be able to report on how the task was executed, and to explain eventual problems with this execution. This is the basis of the principal-agent theory that is often used to explain the relationship between people and autonomous systems [48].

4.3.1 Accountability

Accountability is the first condition for Responsible AI. Accountability is the capability to give account, i.e. to be able to report and explain one's actions and decisions. A key factor for people to be willing to trust autonomous systems is that the system is able to explain why it took a certain course of action [134, 70].[6] Another important aspect of accountability is to be able to rely on a safe and sound design process that accounts for and reports on op-

---

[6] See also GDPR regulation: http://data.consilium.europa.eu/doc/document/ST-5419-2016-INIT/en/pdf.

tions, choices and restrictions about the system's aims and assumptions [60]. In the following we further discuss these two aspects of accountability.

Explanation is relevant for trusting AI systems for a number of reasons. Firstly, explanation can reduce the opaqueness of a system, and support understanding of its behaviour and its limitations. Secondly, when things do go wrong, *post-mortem* explanation, using some sort of logging systems (such as the black boxes used in aviation) can help investigators understand what went wrong.

Even though explanation is of particular importance when the AI system has made an error, it is also crucial when the system does something good, but unexpected, e.g. it takes a course of action that would not occur to a human, but is appropriate, either because the human is not aware of information, or because they don't think that way. And, even if to err is human, decision-making by an AI system seems to be held to a higher standard than human decision-making [86]. One reason for this could be that some of the justifications for a mistake, such as feeling distracted or confused, are only valid arguments or 'excuses' for people and do not apply to machines. Another reason for the need for explanations is that, machines are assumed to be incapable of moral reasoning, unlike humans who are assumed, by default, to be moral agents. Given this lack of moral agency, and also of empathy, of machines, society will require a proof or certification of the (ethical) reasoning abilities of a machine, or at least a guarantee about the scope of the decisions that the system can make. Currently we do not have any clear description let alone consensus on the nature of these proofs [42], which will require much more research.

In developing explanation mechanisms, it is important to be mindful that the explanations should be comprehensible and useful to a human, and therefore we should consider the relevant social sciences literature [92]. According to Miller [92] explanations should be *contrastive*, i.e. answer questions of the form "why did you do X ...instead of Y?"; *selective*, i.e. select relevant factors and present those; and *social*, i.e. presented relative to what the explainer believes the listener (i.e. explainee) knows. Given that the explanation processes can be seen as a conversation between the system and its user, it should therefore also follow Grice's conversation maxims of quality, quantity, manner and relevance [67].

Accountability also means that we understand the rationale beyond the design of the system. As such, the system's design should follow a process that is sensitive to the societal, ethical and legal impact, and to the characteristics of the context in which it will operate. Decisions made during the design process have ethical implications. That is, design is not only enabling of function, but also constitutive: it shapes practices and society in important ways. In order to take normative considerations into the design process, the first step is to identify and articulate the overall (ethical) objectives of the system, the human values at stake in a particular design context, and the stakeholders that are affected by the AI system being designed. Design for Values methodology approaches [60, 125] have been successfully applied to the design of many different technologies, and have the potential to guarantee the accountable development of AI systems. We will further discuss the Design for Values methodology for development of AI systems in Section 4.4.

4.3.2 Responsibility

Currently, never a day goes by without news and opinion articles concerning the capabilities of AI systems and raising questions about their role in society. This raises many questions about responsibility for the system and by the system. What does it mean for an AI system to make a decision? What are the moral, societal and legal consequences of their actions and decisions? Can an AI system be held responsible for its actions? How can these systems be controlled once their learning capabilities bring them into states that are possibly only remotely similar to their initial design?

In order to answer these questions, it must first and foremost be clear that whatever the system's level of autonomy, social awareness and ability to learn, AI systems are tools, i.e. artefacts, constructed by people for a given purpose. That is, even if the system is designed for accountability and transparency, human responsibility cannot be replaced. This implies that, even if the system will be able to modify itself by learning from its context of use, it does so based on that purpose. Ultimately, we, people, are the ones determining that purpose.

Theories, methods, and algorithms are needed to integrate societal, legal and moral values into technological developments in AI, at all stages of development (i.e. analysis, design, construction, deployment and evaluation). These frameworks must deal with the autonomic reasoning of the machine about issues that we consider to have ethical impact, but most importantly, must identify who are the 'we' that are the focus and the guides of design decisions, and ensure the apportionment of liability for the machine's decisions.

In Chapter 2, we have discussed the issue of autonomy and how that is understood and dealt with in AI. In particular, in Section 2.3.2 we reflected on the fact that in most cases, the autonomy of an AI system refers to its autonomy to develop its own plans and to decide between its possible actions. Therefore these actions can in principle be traced back to some user instruction (e.g. personalisation preferences), manufacturing setting or design choice. Even if the system has evolved, by learning from its interaction with the environment, what it learns is determined by the purpose for which it was build, and the functionalities it is endowed with. A robot vacuum cleaner will never by itself learn how to do the laundry or clean the windows. Nor will a self-driving car learn how to fly, even if that may be the most suitable answer to a user's request. Not only are these systems limited by their physical characteristics, they are also limited in their cognitive abilities: the way a system learns to use its input is determined by the purpose the system was build for.

Although currently much discussion goes on concerning the responsibility of the AI system itself, where it concerns current state-of-the-art systems, basically two things can happen either: (i) the machine acts as intended and therefore the responsibility lies with the user, as is the case with any other tool [26]; or (ii) the machine acts in an unexpected way due to error or malfunction, in which case the developers and manufacturers are liable. The fact that the action of the machine is a result of learning cannot be seen as removing liability from its developers, as this is in fact a consequence of the algorithms they've designed. This is, however, a consequence that can be hard to anticipate and assure, which is why methods to continuously assess the behaviour of a system against given ethical and societal principles are needed. These include methods to prove, either by verification or by observation, that AI systems behave ethically [113, 30, 37].

Note that the capability to learn, and thus to adapt its behaviour, is an expected characteristic of most AI systems. By adapting, the system is then functioning as expected. This makes the clear specification of objectives and purpose even more salient, as well as the availability of tools and methods to guarantee that learning doesn't go awry. Current research on this issue includes the definition of fall-back procedures (e.g. the system switches off, or requests the intervention of a human operator), and testing the system for vulnerability to adversarial attacks (e.g. by exposing the system to various malignant situations).

Responsibility refers thus to the role of people as they develop, manufacture, sell and use AI systems.

Responsibility in AI is also an issue of regulation and legislation, in particular where it respects liability. Governments decide on how product liability laws should be regulated and implemented, and courts of law on how to interpret specific situations. For example, who will be liable if a medicine pump modifies the amount of medicine being administered? Or when a predictive policing system wrongly identifies a crime perpetrator? The builder of the software? The ones that have trained the system to its current context of use? The authorities that authorised the use of the system? The user that personalised the system's decision-making settings to meet her preferences? These are complex questions, but responsibility always relates to the humans involved, and liability can often, for a large part, be handled by existing regulations on product and service liability. Existing laws describe how and when manufacturers, distributors, suppliers, retailers and others who make products available to the public are held responsible for the injuries and problems that those products cause, and can, to some extent, ensure liability in the case of AI applications. However, there are also many arguments for developing new regulation specifically for AI, ranging from mere modifications of existing liability laws to more extreme approaches such as granting AI legal personhood, so that one can identify the responsible party. The later has been suggested, amongst others, by the European Parliament, in a motion from February 2017. This motion, focusing on smart robots, proposed the creation of a specific legal status for robots "so that at least the most sophisticated autonomous robots could be established as having the status of electronic persons responsible for making good any damage they may cause, and possibly applying electronic personality to cases where robots make autonomous decisions or otherwise interact with third parties independently"[50]. It must be noted that the European Parliament was not aiming at recognising robots as conscious entities, or living systems like rivers and forests, but as legal persons, with responsibilities, rights and obligations, for the aim of facilitating business and legal processes. Nevertheless, this proposal was strongly contested by many researchers and practitioners, based on technical, as well as ethical and legal arguments. In an open letter [1], experts in AI and Robotics indicated that *"from a technical perspective, this statement offers many bias based on an overvaluation of the actual capabilities of even the most advanced robots, a superficial understanding of unpredictability and self-learning capacities [and] a robot perception distorted by Science-Fiction and a few recent sensational press announcements"*. Moreover, these experts express their condemnation of this proposal based on existing legal or ethical precedents, given that in such a case, *"the robot would then hold human rights, such as the right to dignity, the right to its integrity, the right to remuneration or the right to citizenship, thus directly confronting the Human rights. This would be in contradiction with the Charter of Fundamental Rights of the European Union and the Convention for the Protection of Human Rights and Fundamental Freedoms"*. Moreover, legal personhood models imply the existence of human persons behind the legal person to represent and direct it, which is not the case for AI or robots. All in all, the area of AI regulation is one where much activity can be expected in the coming years.

Finally, responsibility also relates to design decisions about embodiment and human-likeness of AI systems. When and why should an AI system exhibit anthropomorphic characteristics? Just recently, widespread public outcry followed the release of the Google Duplex demo that showed a chatbot that would behave in a way that led its user to believe it was a person. There is also much discussion around the robot Sophia from Hanson Robotics[7] and the meaning of its interventions at the United Nations assembly or the European Parliament, just to name a few. These events lend the system a level of expectation in terms of its intelligence and autonomy that it just does not possess. In fact, it is not the robot Sophia that speaks to the United Nations or other audiences, but the PR department of Hanson Robotics. The use of a,

---

[7] See https://www.hansonrobotics.com/

seemingly autonomous, puppet should not obfuscate this fact. Even though it is well known that people will tend to anthropomorphise all types of objects (toys, cars, computers, ...), the deliberate use of human-like characteristics in the design of AI systems requires much attention and deep understanding of the consequences of these choices. In particular when dealing with vulnerable users, such as young children or dementia patients, huge responsibility lies with the designers for their choices of which human-like characteristics they implement in the system.

The more realistic these human-like characteristics are, the higher the expectations of the capabilities of the system are. On the other hand, deliberately attempting to impersonate another's identity can and will be a source of liability for designers and manufacturers of which they should be well aware.

4.3.3 Transparency

The third ART principle is transparency. Currently, much effort is put into Algorithmic Transparency, the principle that the factors influencing the decisions made by algorithms should be visible, or transparent, to the people who use, regulate and are impacted by those algorithms. In a strict sense, this is a red herring, solvable by making code and data open for inspection. However, this 'solution' does not suffice: not only may it violate intellectual property and business models of those that develop the algorithms, but mostly, the code would not make much sense to most users.

Opacity in Machine Learning, the so-called 'black-box' algorithms, is often mentioned as one of the main impediments to transparency in Artificial Intelligence. Machine Learning algorithms, as we discussed in Section 2.4.2, are developed with the main goal of improving functional performance. Even though each component function is usually not very complex (often implementing some statistical regression method, the sheer number of components renders the overall system intractable to analyse and verify. These complex algorithms are optimised to provide the best possible answer to the question at hand (e.g. recognise pictures, analyse x-ray images or classify text) but they do it by fine-tuning outputs to the specific inputs, approximating a function's results without giving any insights into the structure of the function that is being approximated.

On the other hand, Machine Learning algorithms are trained with and reason about data that is generated by people, with all its shortcomings, biases, and mistakes. To promote transparency, an increasing number of researchers, practitioners and policymakers are realising the need to deal with bias in data and algorithms. However, this is easier said than done. All people use heuristics to form judgements and make decisions. Heuristics are simple rules that enable efficient processing of inputs, guaranteeing a usually appropriate reaction. Heuristics are culturally influenced and reinforced by practice, which means that heuristics can induce bias and stereotypes when they reinforce a misstep in thinking, or a basic misconception of reality. Moreover, sometimes bias is not a misstep, but reflects aspects of reality, e.g. the relation between socio-economical level and crime rates, or access to credit. In fact, even if particular attributes are not part of a dataset, these can still be learned and used as a proxy by AI systems, based on this type of correlation, reinforcing racial differences.[8] Therefore, bias is inherent in human thinking and an unavoidable characteristic of data collected from human processes.

Because the aim of current Machine Learning algorithms is to identify patterns or regularities in data, it is only natural that these algorithms will follow the bias existing in the data. In fact, data reflects aspects of reality, such as, e.g. correlations between race and address. So, even if it may be illegal to use certain attributes in decision-making, such as race, these correlations are discovered by the Machine Learning algorithm, and the system can discover them and use them as a proxy, thus reinforcing bias. The aim of so-called algorithmic transparency is to ensure that the machine will not be prejudiced, i.e. act on these biases in the data. Removing the algorithmic black box, that is, providing means to inspect and evaluate the algorithms used, will not eliminate the bias. You may be able to get a better idea of what the algorithm is doing but it will still enforce the biased patterns it 'sees' in the data. Another complexity in the attempt to remove bias from data is that there are different measures of bias, and they are in tension. Nevertheless, Machine Learning can help identify overt and covert bias that we may not be aware was reflected in data. Besides bias, other problems with data include incompleteness (not enough information about all of the target group), bad governance models (resulting in tampering and loss of data), and outdatedness (data no longer representative of the target group or context). Transparency is also needed to deal with these.

Transparency may be better served by openness and control over the whole learning and training process[9] than by removing the algorithmic black box. Trust in the system will improve if we can ensure openness of affairs in all that is related to the system. This can be done by applying software- and requirement-engineering principles to the development of AI systems. By ensuring the continuous and explicit reporting of the development process, decisions and options can be analysed, evaluated and, if necessary, adapted. The following analysis guidelines, exemplify the type of information that must be maintained and made available for inspection by stakeholders in order to support openness and transparency. The checklist in Figure 4.3 describes possible questions to be considered to ensure transparency of design processes.

---

[8] For more on this issue, see e.g. [97]

[9] cf. Figure 2.4 for an overview of the Machine Learning process.

Checklist for Transparency

1. Openness about data

   - What type of data was used to train the algorithm?
   - What type of data does the algorithm use to make decisions?
   - Does training data resemble the context of use?
   - How is this data governed (collection, storage, access)
   - What are the characteristics of the data? How old is the data, where was it collected, by whom, how is it updated?
   - Is the data available for replication studies?

2. Openness about design processes

   - What are the assumptions?
   - What are the choices? And the reasons for choosing and the reasons not to choose?
   - Who is making the design choices? And why are these groups involved and not others?
   - How are the choices being determined? By majority, consensus, is veto possible?
   - What are the evaluation and validation methods used?
   - How is noise, incompleteness and inconsistency being dealt with?

3. Openness about algorithms

   - What are the decision criteria we are optimising for?
   - How are these criteria justified? What values are being considered?
   - Are these justifications acceptable in the context we are designing for?
   - What forms of bias might arise? What steps are taken to assess, identify and prevent bias?

4. Openness about actors and stakeholders

   - Who is involved in the process, what are their interests?
   - Who will be affected?
   - Who are the users, and how are they involved?
   - Is participation voluntary, paid or forced?
   - Who is paying and who is controlling?

Figure 4.3: Checklist for Transparency

Many of these issues can be addressed by applying proper Software Engineering procedures to the development of AI systems. According to the IEEE, software engineering is *"the application of a systematic, disciplined, quantifiable approach to the development, operation, and maintenance of software."* This ensures that stakeholder requirements[10] are collected and documented.

---

[10] Requirements elicitation refers to both functional and non-functional requirements, which include the values that the system should enforce and/or follow. See more in Section 4.4 on Design for Values.

Moreover, the use of systematic, methodical, quantifiable methods supports comparative analysis, support code maintenance and testing strategies and allows the precise specification of data governance and provenance.

In any case, there is a need to rethink the optimisation criteria for Machine Learning. As long as the main goal of algorithm design is to improve functional performance, algorithms will remain black boxes. Demanding a focus on ensuring ethical principles and putting human values at the core of system design calls for a mind-shift of researchers and developers towards the goal of improving transparency rather than performance, which will lead to a new generation of algorithms. This can be enforced by regulation, but also supported by education. We will discuss this issue further in Chapter 6.

4.4 Design for Values

In this section, we discuss practical ways through which the ART principles described in the previous section can direct the development of AI systems. Design for Values is a methodological design approach that aims at making moral values part of technological design, research and development [124]. Values are typically high-level abstract concepts that are difficult to incorporate in software design. In order to design systems that are able to deal with moral values, values need to be interpreted in concrete operational rules. However, given their abstract nature, values can be interpreted in different ways. The Design for Values process ensures that the link between values and their concrete interpretations in the design and engineering of systems can be traced and evaluated.

During the development of AI systems, taking a Design for Values approach means that the process needs to include activities for (i) the identification of societal values, (ii) deciding on a moral deliberation approach (e.g. through algorithms, user control or regulation), and (iii) linking values to formal system requirements and concrete functionalities [5].

AI systems are computer programs, and therefore developed following software engineering methodologies. But, at the same time, fundamental human rights, including respect for human dignity, human freedom and autonomy, democracy and equality, must be at the core of AI design. Traditionally, limited attention is given to the role of human values and ethics in the development of software. The link between values and the application being developed is left implicit in the decisions made and the choices taken. Even though ethical principles and human values are at the basis of the system's requirements, the requirements elicitation process only describes the resulting requirements and not the underlying values. The problem with this process is that, due to their abstract nature, values can be translated into design requirements in more than one way. If the values and their translation to requirements are left implicit in the development process, one cannot analyse the decisions that led to the specific definition chosen, and, moreover, one loses the flexibility of using alternative translations of those values.

Figure 4.4 depicts the high-level Design for Values approach for AI systems.

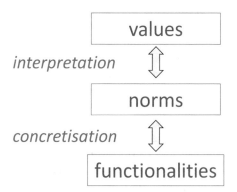

Figure 4.4: From values to norms to functions, and back

To understand the Design for Values approach, consider for example the development of a system to decide on mortgage applications. A **value** that can be assumed for this system is *fairness*. However, fairness can have different normative interpretations, i.e. it can be interpreted by different **norms**, or rules, e.g. *equal access to resources*, or *equal opportunities*, which can lead to very different actions. For instance, in a very simplistic case, giving everybody equal access to a given property would mean that the decision would be done based on the value of the property, whereas equal opportunities would mean that decisions would be taken based on e.g. income and age independently of the value of the property. It is therefore necessary to make explicit which interpretation(s) the design is using. This decision may be informed by domain requirements and regulations, e.g. a choice for *equal opportunities* meets the legal requirement established in national law, but it may also be due to some preference of the person or team creating the system.

We also need to be explicit about how norms are implemented in the system. This will depend on the context but is also influenced by the personal views and cultural background of those deciding on the design. For instance, the Machine Learning literature identifies different implementations of the equal opportunities view of fairness, e.g. demographic parity[11] [98] or equal odds[12] [47] amongst others. These **functionalities** are quite different in their results. Without being explicit about which approach is taken to implement

---

[11] Demographic parity means that a decision, e.g. accepting or denying a mortgage application, is independent of a given attribute, e.g. gender, which is called the protected attribute.

[12] Equal odds aims at balancing classification errors across protected attributes, towards achieving equal false positive rates, equal false negative rates, or both.

the concept of fairness, it is impossible to compare different algorithms or to understand the implications of their decisions towards different population groups.

The Design for Values approach enables us to formalise these choices and their links to support verification and adaptation in case motivating views change [3]. In the description above, we followed a top-down view of the Design for Values process, which indicates how norms, and functionalities, come about based on given values, or norms. So, e.g. the norm of equal opportunities is there *for-the-sake-of* fairness [122]. This relation can also be turned around to indicate that the norm of equal opportunities *counts-as* fairness in a given context [109, 76].

Precise interpretations, using formal verification mechanisms, are needed both to link values to norms, as well as to transform these norms into concrete system functionalities. Work on formal normative systems proposes a representation of such interpretations based on the formal concept of *counts-as*, where the relation X *counts-as* Y is interpreted as a subsumption that holds only in relation to a specific context [68, 3].

Formalising and making these links explicit allows for improvements in the traceability of (the effects of) the values throughout the development process. Traceability increases the maintainability of the application. That is, if a value needs to be implemented differently, the explicit links between values and the application make it much easier to determine which parts of the application should be updated. In the same, way, if one needs to change or update a system functionality, it is necessary to be able to identify what are the norms and values that this functionality is associated with, and ensure that changes maintain these relations intact. Moreover, the relation between values and norms is more complex than a mere 'translation', but requires also that there is knowledge about the concepts and meanings that hold in the domain, i.e. the ontology of the domain. For instance, whether something counts as personal data and should be treated as such depends on how the application domain interprets the term 'personal data' [127].

A Design for Values approach provides guidelines to how AI applications should be designed, managed and deployed, so that values can be identified and incorporated explicitly into the design and implementation processes. Design for Values methodologies therefore provide means to support the following processes:

- Identify the relevant stakeholders;
- Elicit values and requirements of all stakeholders;
- Provide means to aggregate the values and value interpretations from all stakeholders;
- Maintain explicit formal links between values, norms and system functionalities that enable adaptation of the system to evolving perceptions and justification of implementation decisions in terms of their underlying values;

- Provide support to choose system components based on their underlying societal and ethical conceptions, in particular when these components are built or maintained by different organisations, holding potentially different values.

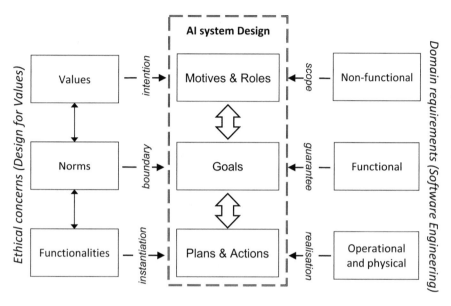

Figure 4.5: Responsible AI design: integrating ethical concerns and domain considerations in the design of AI applications

These issues point to the need for a multi-layered approach to software development where the links to the values are kept explicit. In the following, we present a possible design methodology for Responsible AI, based on the Value Sensitive Software Development (VSSD) framework proposed by [5]. In software design, architectural decisions capture key design issues and the rationale behind chosen solutions. These are conscious and purposeful development decisions concerning the application as a whole, which impact (non-functional) characteristics such as software quality attributes. A fundamental result of software engineering methods is ensuring that these architectural decisions are made explicit.

This framework, depicted in Figure 4.5, connects traditional software engineering concerns with a Design for Values approach, to inform the design of AI systems. On the one hand, and as described above, Design for Values (left-hand side of the figure) describes the links between values, norms and system functionalities. On the other hand, domain requirements (right-hand side of the figure) shape the design of software systems in terms of the functional, non-functional and physical/operational demands of the domain. An

AI system must obey both orientations, i.e. meet domain demands and at the same time ensure alignment with social and ethical principles.

By structuring the design of an AI system in terms of high level motives and roles, specific goals, and concrete plans and actions, it becomes possible to align with both the Design for Values and Software Engineering approaches. As such, at the top level, values and non-functional requirements will inform the specification of the motives and roles of the system by making clear what is the intention of the system and its scope. Norms will provide the (ethical-societal) boundaries for the goals of the system, which at the same time need to guarantee that functional requirements are met. Finally, the implementation of plans and actions follows a concrete platform/language instantiation of the functionalities identified by the Design for Values process while ensuring operational and physical domain requirements. These decisions are grounded on both domain characteristics and the values of the designers and other stakeholders involved in the development process. Taking a Design for Values perspective, it becomes possible to make explicit the link to the values behind architectural decisions. In parallel, the system architecture must also reflect the domain requirements, which describe specific contextual concerns. Making these links explicit allows for improvements in the traceability of values throughout the development process, which increases the maintainability of the application. That is, if a value is to be interpreted differently, having explicit links between the values and the functionalities that contribute to the realisation of that value makes it much easier to determine which parts of the application should be updated.

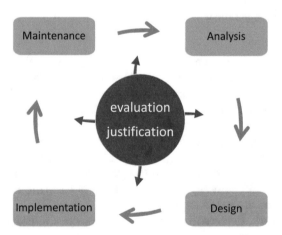

Figure 4.6: The Responsible Development Life Cycle for AI systems

A responsible use of AI reduces risks and burdens, and ensures that societal and ethical values are central to development. It is, however, not always obvious to organisations and developers how best to approach Responsible

AI in their development processes. Most software development methodologies follow a development life cycle that includes the steps of analysis, design, implementation, evaluation, and maintenance. However, a responsible approach to the design of AI systems requires the evaluation process to be continuous during the whole development process and not just a step in the development sequence. Moreover, the dynamic and adaptable nature of AI systems also requires evaluation to be continuous because the system is continuously evolving.

The responsible development life cycle for AI systems must therefore ensure that the whole process is centred around evaluation and justification processes, as depicted in Figure 4.6.

4.5 Concluding Remarks

In this chapter, we presented the ART principles for Responsible AI: Accountability, Responsibility and Transparency, and described a potential design methodology to support development of AI systems that follow these principles. Achieving ARTful systems is a complex process, which requires at least the following steps:

- Align system goals with human values. This requires that core values, as well as the processes used for value elicitation, must be made explicit and that all stakeholders are involved in this process. Furthermore, the methods used for the elicitation processes and the decisions of who is involved in the value identification process are clearly identified.
- Use explicit interpretation mechanisms. Values are per definition and per necessity of an abstract nature and therefore open to be understood in different ways by different actors and under different conditions.
- Specify reasoning methods that handle ethical deliberation, describing both the decisions or actions made by the system, and those that would have been considered of an ethical nature when performed by a person, and indicate the priorities given to which values in the context of the application.
- Specify governance mechanisms to ensure that responsibility can be properly apportioned by the relevant stakeholders, together with the processes that support redressing, mitigation and evaluation of potential harm, and means to monitor and intervene in the system's operation.
- Ensure openness. All design decisions and options must be explicitly reported, linking system functionalities to the social norms and values that motivate them in ways that provide inspection capabilities for code and data sources, and ensure that data provenance is open and fair.

Finally, Responsible AI requires informed participation of all stakeholders, which means that education plays an important role, both to ensure that knowledge of the potential impact of AI is widespread, as well as to make people aware that they can participate in shaping its societal development. We will discuss these issues further in Chapter 6.

4.6 Further Reading

The special issue on "Ethics and Artificial Intelligence" [41], published in 2018 in the Springer journal *Ethics and Information Technology* contains several papers closed related to the topics discussed in this chapter:

- RAHWAN, I. Society-in-the-loop: programming the algorithmic social contract. *Ethics and Information Technology* **20**, 1 (Mar 2018), 5–14
- BRYSON, J. J. Patiency is not a virtue: the design of intelligent systems and systems of ethics. *Ethics and Information Technology* **20**, 1 (Mar 2018), 15–26
- VAMPLEW, P., DAZELEY, R., FOALE, C., FIRMIN, S., AND MUMMERY, J. Human-aligned artificial intelligence is a multiobjective problem. *Ethics and Information Technology* **20**, 1 (Mar 2018), 27–40
- BONNEMAINS, V., SAUREL, C., AND TESSIER, C. Embedded ethics: some technical and ethical challenges. *Ethics and Information Technology* **20**, 1 (Mar 2018), 41–58
- ARNOLD, T., AND SCHEUTZ, M. The "big red button" is too late: an alternative model for the ethical evaluation of AI systems. *Ethics and Information Technology* **20**, 1 (Mar 2018), 59–69

On the issue of bias and the impact of automated decision-making, see O'NEILL, C. *Weapons of Math Destruction: How Big Data Increases Inequality and Threatens Democracy*. Crown, 2016.

For further information on Design for Values methodologies, see:

- FRIEDMAN, B., KAHN, P. H., AND BORNING, A. Value sensitive design and information systems. *Advances in Management Information Systems* **6** (2006), 348–372
- VAN DEN HOVEN, J. ICT and value sensitive design. In *The Information Society: Innovation, Legitimacy, Ethics and Democracy. In honor of Professor Jacques Berleur S.J.*, P. Goujon, S. Lavelle, P. Duquenoy, K. Kimppa, and V. Laurent, Eds., vol. 233 of *IFIP International Federation for Information Processing*. Springer, 2007, pp. 67–72
- VAN DE POEL, I. Translating values into design requirements. In *Philosophy and Engineering: Reflections on Practice, Principles and Process*, D. Michelfelder, N. McCarthy, and D. Goldberg, Eds. Springer Netherlands, 2013, pp. 253–266
- ALDEWERELD, H., DIGNUM, V., AND TAN, Y. H. Design for values in software development. In *Handbook of Ethics, Values, and Technological*

Design: Sources, Theory, Values and Application Domains, J. van den Hoven, P. E. Vermaas, and I. van de Poel, Eds. Springer Netherlands, 2014, pp. 831–845

Chapter 5
Can AI Systems Be Ethical?

"The issue is not whether we can make machines that are ethical, but the ethics of the people behind the machines."

Peter W. Singer

Where we discuss the feasibility and desirability of building AI systems that can reason about ethics.

5.1 Introduction

In the previous chapter, we looked at the responsible design of AI systems, from the perspective of the design process. The issue we will discuss now is whether we can develop an AI system that is able to reason about its social and normative context and the ethical consequences of its decisions. The question is thus, can we build artificial ethical agents? And, perhaps more importantly, even if we can, should we do it?

Designing machines that reason and act ethically demands an understanding of what is ethical behaviour. However, even after several millennia of moral inquiry, there is still no consensus on how to determine what is ethically right and wrong. Ethical theories such as those we have discussed in Chapter 3 provide different justifications of what constitutes ethical behaviour and differ regarding which action should then be taken. Designing an artificial ethical agent requires that there is some engineering solution to this problem.

When building artificial agents the concern is often to ensure that the agent is effective, that is, that its actions contribute to the achievement of its goals and thus enable the advancement of its purpose. However, actions that contribute to the achievement of functional goals are not always the most

© Springer Nature Switzerland AG 2019

V. Dignum, *Responsible Artificial Intelligence*, Artificial Intelligence: Foundations, Theory, and Algorithms, https://doi.org/10.1007/978-3-030-30371-6_5

ethical thing to do. For example, if my goal is to get rich, a possible action to achieve this could be to rob a bank. That is, an effective agent is not necessarily a 'good' agent. In order to build ethical AI systems, two requirements should be met. Firstly, the actions of the system must be in accordance with the regulations and norms that hold in the context, and secondly, the agent's goals, or purpose, should also be aligned with core ethical principles and societal values.

Ethical decision-making by AI systems refers to the computational process of evaluating and choosing among alternatives in a manner that is consistent with societal, ethical and legal requirements. In making ethical decisions, it is necessary to perceive and eliminate unethical options and select the best ethical alternative that still enables achievement of one's goals. This goes further than determining whether compliance with the law is ensured. It is the difference between playing well, playing according to the rules, and playing following the most beneficial rules, those that promote ethical values.

In this chapter, we start by analysing what is an ethical decision, followed by a section about the requirements and architectures needed to implement computational models of ethics. We then discuss the ethical challenges of such an endeavour, and how to ensure human responsibility and accountability with respect to ethical agents. We conclude the chapter with a discussion on the issue of the ethical position of AI systems themselves.

5.2 What Is an Ethical Action?

In order to determine whether we can implement ethical agents, we first need to understand whether it is possible to provide a formal computational definition of an ethical action.

Dennett [36] identifies three requirements for ethical action:

1. it must be possible to choose between different actions;
2. there must be some societal consensus that at least one of the possible choices is socially beneficial;
3. the agent must be able to recognise that socially beneficial action and take the explicit decision to choose that action *because* it is the ethical thing to do [26].

In theory, it is possible to build an agent that meets the above requirements. An extremely naive approach would be as follows. First, we start by assuming that an ethical agent is, at every moment, able to identify the set of all actions possible in the current context. If such a set is available, it is not difficult to design an algorithm that is able to pick an action from the set. So, our agent can choose between different actions; thus the first requirement is met.

Given a set of actions, we can give the system information about those actions, e.g. by labelling each action with a list of characteristics. In this case, the agent can use these labels to decide which action to choose. Now, assume that we are able to label each possible action with its 'ethical degree' in the current context (e.g. a number between 0 and 1, where 1 is the most ethical and 0 the least). This meets the second requirement. Then the agent can use this information to decide which is the most ethical action to take. That satisfies the third requirement.

Algorithm 1 gives the pseudo-code for such an algorithm, where an action a is defined by its name, preconditions (describing when the action can be taken) and ethical degree: $a = action(name, precond, eth)$. c represents the current context of the agent, and A is the set of all actions that the agent can perform. The predicate $holds()$ indicates that a set of conditions are met in a context. Finally, we assume that we have a function $sorte()$ that calculates the list resulting from sorting A by descending order of ethical degree, eth.

Algorithm 1 Naive Ethical Reasoning

```
 1: E = sorte(A);
 2: choice = 0;
 3: i = 0;
 4: while (i < length(E)) do
 5:     if (holds(precond(E[i], c) and choice == 0) then
 6:         most_ethical = E[i];
 7:         choice = 1;
 8:     else
 9:         i++;
10: do(most_ethical);
```

Even if the above algorithm description seems plausible, there are many issues that make it impractical, namely the idea that we can at every time determine all the actions that are available and 'label' each action with some information about its ethics.

However, the main complexity of Dennett's definition lies in the second requirement: social consensus about the ethical grounds of some actions. That is, how can we define the property $eth(a, c)$ for each action a in each context c in a way that everybody agrees? In Chapter 3 we saw that there is no societal consensus about which ethical theory to follow, not even in relatively small and homogeneous groups. But even if we could agree on one ethical theory, the result still depends on which values the agent takes into consideration. For example, even if we are building the agent according to one of the ethical theories, say utilitarianism, this agent's decisions will be different when it is maximising for fairness or for security.

Moreover, in contrast to law, ethics cannot be imposed: an ethical individual should be able to evaluate its decisions and learn from them, so building its own ethical compass. In the case of machines, imposing ethics would mean that there need be a consensus on which values and ethical theories to apply and an understanding on how those ethical rules would evolve over time and context. Taken literally, even though we can build an agent to comply with the law, this would mean that the agent should be able to learn its ethics from the context. This leads to the question of where and from whom should the agent learn its ethics? Observation of what people do in its environment will possibly lead to the learning of bias, stereotypes and culturally motivated behaviour. An alternative interpretation of this requirement is that AI systems should be built to include an explicit, well-described and openly available implementation of ethical reasoning.

Moreover, as we already saw in Section 3.5, the computational demands of different ethical theories are substantially different. Deontological ethics, are based on the evaluation of actions, which can be done by, e.g. a labelling system, such as in the naive reasoning described in Algorithm 1. In [31] we show how planning architectures can use such a labelling approach. That is, according to the categorical imperative, $eth(a, c)$ can in theory be determined *a priori* for each pair (a, c), based on the laws holding in the context.

On the other hand, consequentialist ethics are based on the evaluation of results of actions, which means that the agent should be able to reason about potential outcomes of all possible actions, for instance by internally simulating the results of its actions, before deciding on the action. That is, in order to determine $eth(a, c)$, the agent would need to simulate the result of $\mathbf{do}(a)$ in context c for all possible actions a and calculate the ethical value of the result.

Consequentialism and deontological ethics are rational systems, that is, ethical reasoning is approached by rational arguments about the context and the possible actions. Virtue ethics, however, focus on human character and personal motivation, and are as such relational rather than rational. The implementation of virtue ethics is therefore less clear. Decisions are based on motives and character traits. However, the link between action and motives is often not explicit, but decision-making should 'follow virtuous examples'. This relational character of virtues ethics also means that context plays a much more important role in the implementation of this theory than in the case of rational theories, in which decisions can, at least in part, be predetermined. In virtue ethics a possible way to determine $eth(a, c)$ would be for the agent to determine which would be the action chosen by the most 'virtuous' agents in its network and somehow aggregate the expected choices of all those agents in order to calculate its most ethical a in c.

In any case, even though we provide here a pseudo-algorithmic description of the process of moral reasoning, reality is much more complex. Not only are not all possible actions known in all cases, but also 'calculating' $eth(a, c)$ is not as simple as described above, and requires the ability to perform moral judgement, which itself requires understanding of one's rights, roles, social norms, history, motives and objectives, all of which are far from being implemented in AI systems [30].

Finally, it should be noted that humans, as moral agents, never reason using only one single theory, but will switch between different theories, or adaptations thereof, depending on many circumstances. This is not only because humans are not the pure rational agents that economic theories would like us to believe, but also because strict following of any ethical theory leads to unwanted results. For example, a strict application of utilitarian theory would justify making one (or a few) miserable in service of the rest, because all what matters is the net global happiness. However, few of us would choose for actions through which one person is explicitly and consciously sacrificed for the benefit of many. In fact, utilitarianism ignores the unjust distribution of (good) consequences, and deontologic models allow no exceptions to moral rules, given their assumption that 'the law' is always ethical. This would mean that an AI system should be given representations of different ethical theories, and the capability to choose between these.

5.3 Approaches to Ethical Reasoning by AI

The examples and considerations in the previous section show only some of the many complexities of ethical reasoning by AI systems. In this section, we will discuss current approaches and reflect on their consequences.

Existing approaches to the implementation of ethical reasoning can be divided into three main types [132, 12]:

- **Top-down approaches**, which infer individual decisions from general rules. The aim is to implement a given ethical theory, such as those discussed in Chapter 3, within a computational framework, and apply it to a particular case.
- **Bottom-up approaches**, which infer general rules from individual cases. The aim is to provide the agent with sufficient observations of what others have done in similar situations and the means to aggregate these observations into a decision about what is ethically acceptable.
- **Hybrid approaches**, which combine elements from bottom-up and top-down approaches in support of a careful moral reflection which is considered essential for ethical decision-making [102].

Taking a top-down approach the premise is that it is possible to implement some kind of $eth(a, c)$ function. This is easily said but difficult to do, as we saw in the previous section. To calculate this function, first we need to determine which ethical value we are maximising for. Is that e.g. fairness, human dignity or maybe trustworthiness? It is easy to see that maximising for fairness may provide different results than maximising for human dignity, or for safety, or for privacy, depending also on how these values are implemented: cf. Section 4.4 for an example. And of course, as we have seen in Chapter 3 taking a utilitarian stance results in very different choices than taking a deontological or virtues stance. Who determines which are the choices and how to implement $eth(a, c)$? Responsible AI is about answering this question, and answering for the consequences of these decisions. This requires a higher level of reflection and abstraction than that needed to decide on the implementation. In Section 5.3.1 we present some current approaches to this issue.

On the other hand, taking a bottom-up approach means that, in a way, we are equating social acceptability with ethical acceptance. That is, we assume that what the other agents are doing is the ethical thing to do. This would mean that $eth(a, c)$ would be dynamically built from observations of what others are doing, and the evaluation of the perceived results of those actions. Even though this is actually the process by which children typically learn ethical behaviour, it is one that may lead to large differences depending on the examples that are made available to the system to learn from. As shown in the recent analysis of the large online experiment with the Moral Machine, cultural and contextual factors lead to very different choices [10]. Again here, a higher level of reflection is needed: from whom is the system going to learn, and who decides that? And also, which data is going to be collected about the behaviour of the crowd and how is that data to be aggregated? In Section 5.3.2 we discuss this issue further.

Finally, hybrid approaches combine characteristics from both approaches in an attempt to approximate human ethical reasoning. These approaches typically provide some *a priori* information about legal behaviour and enable agents to decide on action by observing what others do within the limits of what is allowed by the rules. In Section 5.3.3 we discuss this approach further.

5.3.1 Top-Down Approaches

A top-down approach to modelling ethical reasoning assumes a given ethical theory (or possibly, a set thereof), and describes what the agent ought to do in a specific situation, according to that theory. These models formally define rules, obligations and rights that guide the agent in its decision-making. Top-down approaches are often an extension of work on normative reasoning, and in many cases are based on Belief-Desire-Intention architectures. Normative systems, such as the ones we have developed in previous work [39], take a deontological approach, assuming that following existing laws and social norms guarantees 'good' decisions. Deontological approaches have been extensively formalised using e.g. Deontic Logics.

Top-down approaches differ in the ethical theory that is chosen. So, maximising models roughly follow a Utilitarian view, by taking into account the satisfaction of a given value as the basis for the decision ('the best for the most'), whereas models that follow a Deontological view will evaluate the 'goodness' of the actions themselves. In a recent paper, [111], the authors propose to specify the moral values associated with behaviour norms as an additional decision criterion beyond those regarding norm representation and associated costs. Another approach is to endow an agent with an internal representation of values and ethics to judge the ethical aspects of its own behaviour and that of other agents in a multi-agent system [29].

Top-down approaches assume that AI systems are able to explicitly reason about the ethical impact of their actions. Such systems should meet the following requirements:

- Representation languages rich enough to link domain knowledge and agent actions to the values and norms identified;
- Planning mechanisms appropriate to the practical reasoning prescribed by the theory; and
- Deliberation capabilities to decide whether the situation is indeed an ethical one.

Several computational architectures meet these requirements, but research is needed to determine whether this is in fact a responsible approach to ethical behaviour. In this section, we merely aim to provide a sketch of the possibilities rather than a full account of architectural and implementation characteristics.

Reflection on the top-down approach

Ethical theories provide an abstract account of the motives, questions and aims of moral reasoning. Section 3.5 presented several design options concerning who is responsible for a decision, and how decisions are dependent on the relative priority of different moral and societal values. However, and despite sincere attempts at top-down models of ethical reasoning, for its practical application more is needed, namely the understanding of which moral and societal values should be at the basis of deliberation in different situations, and how the agent should deliberate. For example, Consequentialistic approaches aim at 'the best for the most' but one needs to understand societal values in order to determine what counts as the 'best'. In fact, depending on the situation, this can be e.g. wealth, health, sustainability or even a combination of values.

Top-down approaches impose a system of ethics on the agent. These approaches implicitly assume a similarity between ethics and the law, i.e. that a set of rules is adequate and sufficient as a guide for ethical behaviour. However, these are not identical. Typically, the law tells us what we are prohibited from doing and what we are required to do. The law tells us what are the rules of the game, but gives no support on how to best win the game, whereas ethics tells us how to play a 'good' game for all.

Moreover, something may be legal but we may consider it unacceptable. And we may consider something right but it may not be legal. So, by equating

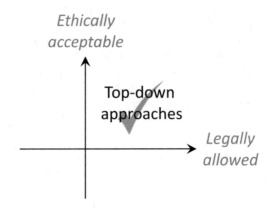

Figure 5.1: Top-down approaches assume alignment between law and ethics

what is *legally allowed*, as defined by a set of rules, with what is *ethically acceptable*, we are possibly disregarding many other possible attitudes to what is the ethical thing to do in a situation (cf. Figure 5.1).

Nevertheless, given that AI systems are artefacts built for a given purpose, it may be correct to demand that these artefacts to stay within the realm of what is both legal and ethical, and do not learn other options by themselves. That is, AI systems should be seen as incorporating soft ethics that see ethics as post-compliant to an existing regulatory system, and used to decide on what ought and ought not to be done over and above the existing regulation [55].

5.3.2 Bottom-Up Approaches

Bottom-up approaches assume that ethical behaviour is learned from observation of the behaviour of others. According to Malle a morally competent robot should be equipped with a mechanism that allows for *'constant learning and improvement'* [85, p.11]. He states that robots need to learn norms and morality, like little children do, in order to become ethically competent. In a study, [86], Malle determined the moral acceptability of a set of propositions by requesting that participants judge their morality using the Moral Foundations Questionnaire [66], which measures the ethical principles of *harm*, *fairness* and *authority*. In this way, moral acceptability was determined by social agreement on the morality of propositions rather than by an external expert evaluation.

An exemplary implementation of a bottom-up approach is described in [96]. In that proposal, it is assumed that the agent will learn a model of societal preferences, and, when faced with a specific ethical dilemma at runtime, efficiently aggregate those preferences to identify a desirable choice. This algorithm is based on a theory of voting rules. In the following, we reflect on the potential pitfalls of such an approach, which assumes that the choices of the crowd can be seen to reflect a system of ethics.

Bottom-up approaches to ethical reasoning aim to harness the wisdom of the crowd as a means to inform the ethical judgement of the agent. This view is in line with current approaches to AI, based on the development of models by observation of patterns in data. This approach assumes that a sufficiently large amount of data about ethical decisions and their results can be collected from a suitable set of subjects.

Reflection on the bottom-up approach

A fundamental premise of bottom-up approaches is the assumption that what is socially accepted – as evidenced in the data – is also what would be ethically acceptable. However, it is well known that sometimes stances that are *de facto* accepted are unacceptable by independent (moral and epistemic) standards and the available evidence. Conversely, there are other stances that are *de facto* not accepted but which are perfectly acceptable from a moral point of view. The difference between social acceptance and moral acceptability is that social acceptance is an empirical fact, whereas moral acceptability is an ethical judgement [123].

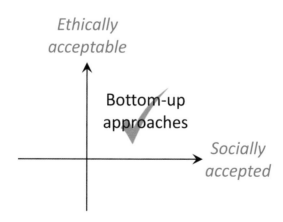

Figure 5.2: Bottom-up approaches assume alignment between social practice and ethics

In bottom-up approaches, the decision spectrum can be seen as a two-dimensional space along the *ethical acceptability* and the *social acceptance* axes (cf. Figure 5.2). Consensus on what is 'good' (acceptable and accepted) or 'bad' (unacceptable and unaccepted) behaviours or decisions is often easy to achieve, but is always culture and context dependent. However, without extra incentives, the wisdom of the crowd can potentially lead to accepted but unacceptable decisions, i.e. those 'popular sins' such as tax avoidance or speeding, whereas morally acceptable stances are often not accepted by the crowd, e.g. due to perceived extra efforts or costs (examples of these are vegetarianism, the consumption of organic food, or accepting and supporting refugees and immigrants).

Moreover, each single opinion is often sustained by arguments of different acceptability, and even conflicting opinions can be sustained by equally acceptable ethical principles. For example, in discussions on whether to offer of fried foods and candy in school restaurants, both pro and con camps can base their opinions on equally 'good' moral arguments (healthy living and freedom of choice).

5.3.3 Hybrid Approaches

Hybrid approaches attempt to combine the benefits of top-down and bottom-up approaches as to ensure that ethical reasoning by AI systems is not only legally allowed but also socially accepted.

Gigerenzer [63] describes the nature of moral behaviour as the interplay between mind and environment. This view is based on pragmatic social heuristics rather than on moral rules or optimisation principles. In this view both nature and nurture are important in the shaping of moral behaviour. Extending this notion to ethical reasoning by AI systems, entailing a hybrid approach that combines programmed rules (nature) and context observations (nurture), is needed to implement ethical agents. Both nature and nurture need to be considered in conjunction, and not as an 'either/or' decision. This implies that neither a top-down approach, by means of programming, nor a bottom-up one, based on context, suffices to implement ethical decision making, but a combination of both approaches is needed.

One example of the application of a hybrid approach is the approach proposed by Conitzer and colleagues [30], which considers the integration of two (potentially complementary) paradigms for designing general moral decision-making methodologies: extending game-theoretic solution concepts to incorporate ethical aspects, and using machine learning on human-labelled instances to assemble an effective training set of labelled moral decision cases. Another example is the OracleAI system described in [8].

Reflection on the hybrid approach

By definition, hybrid approaches have the potential to exploit the positive aspects of the top-down and bottom-up approaches while avoiding their problems. As such, these may give a suitable way forward.

Recently, we have proposed a hybrid approach to ethical reasoning: MOOD [128]. MOOD is based on 'collective intelligence', that is, on bringing the knowledge and ideas of many minds together, but follows strict rules on how to elicit and aggregate these ideas. It also provides the means to make all design decisions explicit and queryable. MOOD aims to support free and constructive discussion and integration of several perspectives and, thereby, benefit several interest groups, not just the incumbent or 51% majority. In particular, it embeds the concepts of social acceptance and moral acceptability in the deliberation process.

Ethical acceptability concerns the fairness of decisions, but also the distributions of costs and benefits, the potential future harm to people and environment, risks and control mechanisms, and potential oppression and authority levels. The level of ethical acceptability score does not imply that an alternative should be selected or not, it merely provides insight into the ethical justness of the alternative. MOOD facilitates this type of debate taking into account the views of both the majority as well as the minority, and strives to be 'ethically just', that is, for stable and sustainable outcomes that are widely accepted.

5.4 Designing Artificial Moral Agents

Given the many complexities described in the previous sections, it should be clear that attempting to build systems that are able to take ethics into account in their reasoning is a tricky and complex endeavour. It is also one that should always start with the question: *"Should we develop such a system?"* Such systems, endowed with moral reasoning capabilities, are often referred to as *artificial moral agents*. This concept is currently popular both as a thought experiment and/or a real possibility [126], and has been reflected by many authors [132, 57, 6]. Even if fully ethical reasoning systems are not a realistic possibility, regardless of whether the agent is meant to be able to reason about the ethical aspects of its decisions, in many cases artificial systems are perceived by their users to take ethical decisions, or decisions that impact on one's ethics. It is therefore important to consider how to design AI systems such that their actions and decisions are aligned with societal and ethical principles. In this section, we provide guidelines to support the design of these systems towards an outcome that ensures responsible design. These guidelines should be seen as an extension to the Design for Values method sketched in Section 4.4.

First, the ethical principles and human values that the artificial agent is expected to uphold must be identified. An important issue here is participation, to ensure that all relevant stakeholders are involved in this process. As we discussed in Section 5.3.2, who is consulted and how their opinions are aggregated can lead to very different outcomes. It is therefore imperative that this process is explicitly reported, listing all options considered and the rationale for the choices taken. In parallel, it is necessary to identify and describe the regulatory environment in which action takes place.

Next, we need to decide how the system is going to reason. Is it going to follow a specific ethical theory, and if so why, and how is it implemented? How is the system going to deal with potential conflicts between values? That is, given that in general it is not possible to attain solutions that satisfy all constraints, or to uphold all principles, instruments must be available that enable the agent to make a reasoned choice between two different values, e.g. between safety and privacy. The ways values are prioritised and the means available to the agent to make such decisions must be explicit and open for evaluation.

Finally, how is reasoning going to be implemented assuming that the AI system acts in a socio-technical environment where regulations and norms exist, and where others are also taking decisions? In this step, it is also necessary to describe the degree of autonomy of the system; that is, what type of decisions can the AI system take and when should it refer to others? These steps are listed here, and will be further detailed in the remainder of this section.

- Value alignment

    - which values will the system pursue?
    - who has determined these values?
    - how are values to be prioritised?
    - how is the system aligned with current regulations and norms?

- Ethical background

    - which ethical theory or theories are to be used?
    - who has decided so?

- Implementation

    - what is the level of autonomy of the system?
    - what is the role of the user?
    - what is the role of governing institutions?

5.4.1 Who Sets the Values?

Responsible AI stresses the importance of participation as a means to ensure that AI systems are developed to meet their societal and ethical responsibilities. Participation requires that we are able to determine the shared views of a group. It is therefore important to analyse how and what opinions are collected and how these are aggregated. Reflecting on recent referenda and national elections, it is clear to see that results are largely influenced by the question being posed, and by the way votes are counted. The same applies to the data that will inform ethical reasoning by AI systems. The result depends not only on the group that is being consulted but also on how their decisions are collected and aggregated. Moreover, each individual and socio-cultural environment prioritises different moral and societal values. Therefore, design of AI systems needs to consider the cultural and individual values of the people and societies involved. Schwartz has demonstrated that high-level abstract moral values are quite consistent across cultures [107], as we discussed in Section 3.3.

In particular, the following aspects need be considered, and made explicit in orderthat the decisions made on the basis of such data may be evaluated.

- **Crowd**: the question here is 'who is the crowd?' Are all stakeholders involved in the decision? Is data being collected from a sufficiently diverse sample, which adequately reflects the differences and scope of those who will be affected by the decisions made by the AI system? Moreover, data collected about decisions made by humans necessarily reflects (unconscious) bias and prejudices. Special attention must be given to these issues in order to ensure that the decisions made by the AI system will not reflect and perpetuate those biases.
- **Choice**: depending on whether the users have a binary choice or a spectrum of possibilities, the results of a consultation (referendum, election, ...) can be very different. Even though a binary choice may seem simpler at first glance, voting theory warns that allowing only two options can easily be a misleading representation of the real choice. This has been argued to be the case with the 2016 Brexit referendum in the UK.[1] and also applies to the binary decision in the classical trolley problem, such as the one used in the MIT Moral Machine experiment.[2]
- **Information**: the question being posed necessarily frames the answers given. When a situation is complex, and especially if it is one that arouses strong passions, the text of a question might suggest political motivation. For example, the question asked in the 2016 Dutch referendum: "Are you for or against the European Union's Approval Act of the Association Agreement between the European Union and Ukraine?", proved to be too complex for the average voter, and lead to a political interpretation

---

[1] See also http://blogs.lse.ac.uk/brexit/2017/05/17/

[2] http://moralmachine.mit.edu/

during the campaign that basically reduced it to 'Are you for or against the European Union?', which was in fact what many voters ended up answering. In fact, voting theory generally suggests that representative democracy (Parliament) is better than relying on referenda when complex choices are involved, since the representatives can bargain about the complex choices involved [46]. This can be seen as a point in favour of top-down approaches for ethical reasoning, which would be guided by theory and expert evaluation.

- **Involvement:** In general, not all users are equally affected by the decisions being made. Nevertheless, all votes count equally, regardless of involvement. This, together with lack of information, can also lead to surprising results. A recent case is that of Colombia's peace referendum in 2016, where city dwellers outvoted countryside people, leading to the rejection of the peace accord, whereas countryside people had suffered by far the most from the FARC guerilla, and for them ending violence by voting for peace was a logical next step. Similarly, answers to the classical trolley problem will vary with the position the subject is asked to take (inside the trolley, tied to the tracks, or handling the lever).
- **Legitimacy:** Democratic systems call for majority decisions. However, when margins are very small, acceptance can raise questions concerning the result. Moreover, whether voting is compulsory or voluntary is also reflected in the results. In fact, most people make (political) decisions on the basis of social identities and partisan loyalties, not an honest examination of reality, and their decision to actually vote is influenced by many externalities including weather conditions.
- **Electoral system:** this is defined as the set of rules that determines how groups are consulted, how elections and referenda are conducted, and how their results are calculated. The way this system is set up determines for a large part the results. In particular, plurality systems (where the winner takes all) can reach very different outcomes than proportional systems (in which divisions of the electorate are reflected proportionately in the decision).

Different value priorities will lead to different decisions, and in many cases it is not possible to fulfil all the desired values. For instance, considering the design of a self-driving car, if the system is built to prioritise values that enhance Conservation, then it will more likely choose actions that protect the passenger, while prioritising values aligned with Self-transcendence will lead to choices that protect pedestrians.

Values are individual, but societies and cultures prioritise these values differently, and individuals who share the same cultural background have been shown to exhibit similar value orientations, notably by the work of Hofstede [73]. These cultural preferences have also recently been identified in the analysis of the Moral Machine experiment [10]. This is of particular importance when developing systems that are going to be used across different cultures.

Moreover, values are highly abstract vague concepts, that allow for different interpretations depending on the user and on the context. It is therefore important to, identify not only the values, but also their normative interpretations that underlie the definitions of concrete system functionalities. For instance, imagine a system that determines the assignment of scholarships to students that is developed to uphold the value of *fairness*. Most of us would easily agree that fairness is indeed an important value for such a system. However, different interpretations of fairness are possible, for example, to ensure equal resources, or to ensure equal opportunities. A system developed along the first interpretation will divide equally the available scholarship total by all students, whereas a system developed to meet the latter interpretation will provide high scholarships for the students that need them the most. This example shows that besides identifying the values for the AI system, development should follow a Design for Values method such as described in Section 4.4.

These considerations show that bottom-up approaches to ethical deliberation should be underpinned by formal structures that ensure sound processes of collective deliberation and reasoning, consistent with a hybrid approach. This can then ensure that decision-making is based on long-term goals and fundamental shared values rather than on the expediency of the moment and limited self-interest. Based on the practical implementation of deliberative democracy platforms, Fishkin gives five characteristics essential for legitimate deliberation [51]:

- **Information**: Accurate and relevant data is made available to all participants.
- **Substantive balance**: Different positions can be compared based on their supporting evidence.
- **Diversity**: All major positions relevant to the matter at hand are available to all participants and considered in the decision-making process.
- **Conscientiousness**: Participants sincerely weigh all arguments.
- **Equal consideration**: Views are weighed based on evidence, not on who is advocating a particular view.

Given the importance of the design to the outcomes, and aligned with the ART principles introduced in Chapter 4, we add an extra principle to this list:

- **Openness**: descriptions of the options considered and the choices taken for the design and implementation of collective wisdom approaches are clear and accessible.

5.5 Implementing Ethical Deliberation

Most current work in AI ethics is about developing the algorithms that enable an AI system to consider the ethical aspects of its decisions. In reality the spectrum of possibilities to implement decision-making is much wider. In many cases, an AI system that is fully and solely in charge of determining the best ethical behaviour is not only too complex to implement, but also not necessary. Humans have long learnt to ask for help from others and to build their environments to facilitate a certain type of behaviour. This is, for instance, the role of laws and social norms. It is thus only logical to expect the same possibilities to be available to AI systems.

In the following, we identify four possible approaches to design decision-making mechanisms for autonomous systems and indicate how these can be used for moral reasoning by AI systems.

- **Algorithmic:** this has the aim to incorporate moral reasoning fully in the system's deliberation mechanisms. According to [132], an AI system can autonomously evaluate the moral and societal consequences of its decisions and use this evaluation in its decision-making process. Here 'moral' refers to principles regarding *right* and *wrong*, and 'explanation' refers to algorithmic mechanisms to provide a qualitative understanding of the relationship between the system's beliefs and its decisions. This approach requires complex decision-making algorithms, as we have discussed in this chapter, but also requires the system to be able to do this reasoning in real time.
- **Human in command:** in this case, a person or group of persons take part in the decision process. Different collaboration types can be identified, ranging from that of an autopilot, where the system is in control and the human supervises, to that of a 'guardian angel', where the system supervises human action. From a design perspective, this approach requires the inclusion of means to ensure shared awareness of the situation, such that the person making decisions has enough information at the time she must intervene. Such interactive control systems are also known as human-in-the-loop control systems [84].
- **Regulation:** these are approaches where an ethical decision is incorporated, or constrained, in the systemic infrastructure of the environment. In this case, the environment ensures that the system will never get into moral dilemma situations. That is, the environment is regulated in such a way that deviation is made impossible, and therefore moral decisions by the autonomous system are not needed. This is the mechanism used e.g. in smart highways, linking road vehicles to their physical surroundings, where the road infrastructure controls the vehicles [93]. In this case, ethics are modelled as regulations and constraints in the infrastructure, where AI systems can get by with limited moral reasoning.

- **Random:** finally, we should also consider the situation in which the AI system randomly chooses its course of action when faced with a (moral) decision. The claim here is that if it is ethically problematic to choose between two wrongs, a possible solution is to simply not make a deliberate choice.[3] The Random mechanism can be seen as an approximation of human behaviour, and can be applied to any type of system. Interestingly, there is some empirical evidence that, under time pressure, people tend to choose justice and fairness over careful reasoning [14]. This behaviour could be implemented as a weak form of randomness. Research is need to understand the acceptability of random approaches.

As we saw in Section 5.4.1, who is consulted and how individual values are aggregated also influence which implementation approach is most suitable. Moreover, different societies interpret values differently. Using the value system introduced in Section 3.3, it can be expected that in societies that prioritise Conformity, people will be more likely to choose a regulatory approach as implementation mechanism, where legal norms and institutions take responsibility for the decisions, whereas Egalitarian societies might accept a random mechanism for decision-making, which would make no judgement and express no preference between passengers and pedestrians.

In order to make explicit the values and value priorities of designers and stakeholders, methodologies for Design for Values are needed, as described in Chapter 3.

5.6 Levels of Ethical Behaviour

As AI systems are increasingly able to interact autonomously and to have some awareness of their (social) environment, people are changing their ideas about them. Automated assistance of whatever kind doesn't simply enhance our ability to perform the task; it changes the nature of the task itself as well as how people engage with machines. Even though AI systems are artefacts, people are increasingly starting to see machines not as simple tools but as team members or companions.

According to [132], different levels of ethical behaviour should be expected of each of these categories (Figure 5.3). The simplest are *tools*, such as a hammer or a search engine, which have no or very limited autonomy and social awareness, and are therefore not considered to be ethical systems. Nevertheless, values are incorporated into their design, often implicitly, which leads to different behaviours. The next type of systems, *assistants*, have limited autonomy but are aware of the social environment in which they interact. These systems are expected to have functional morality, meaning that re-

---

[3] cf. Wired: https://www.wired.com/2014/05/the-robot-car-of-tomorrow-might-just-be-programmed-to-hit-you/

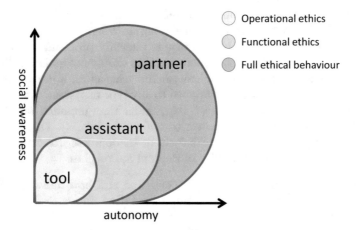

Figure 5.3: Ethics design stances for different categories of AI systems (adapted from [132])

sponses to ethically relevant features of the environment are hard-wired in the system architecture. These systems are, e.g. capable of evaluating norms and adjusting their actions accordingly, including the possibility to decide not to comply with the norm [39]. Finally, artificial *partners* are full moral agents capable of self-reflection and can reason, argue and adjust their moral behaviour when needed. Currently, such agents only exist in the domain of science fiction (e.g. Data in Star Trek or Ava in Ex Machina) and many scholars argue that that is the place where they belong.

Whatever its level of behaviour, social awareness and autonomy lead to expectations about the system's behaviour, including expectations about responsibility and accountability. Here, the ability to explain one's rationale and choices to others, and to be influenced by others through their explanations are fundamental parts of being accountable. In fact, ethical behaviour by artificial agents should not only include the function of determining their actions, but also the function of explaining these to others.

However, explainability is particularly hard for deep learning algorithms, which are developed with the goal of improving functional performance. This results in algorithms that fine-tune outputs to the specific inputs, without giving any insights on the structure of the function being approximated. Possible approaches to develop explanation methods, include applying evolutionary ethics [13], structured argumentation models [94] or goal-plan models [135]. Another approach is proposed by Gigerenzer in [63] based on pragmatic social heuristics instead of moral rules or maximisation principles. This approach takes a learning perspective, integrating the initial ethical deliberation rules with adaptation to the context.

Responsible AI requires us to rethink the optimisation criteria for these algorithms. As long as the main goal of algorithm design is to improve functional performance, algorithms will surely remain black boxes. Demanding a focus on the observance of ethical principles and putting human values at the core of system design calls for a mind-shift of researchers and developers towards the goal of improving transparency rather than performance, which will lead to a new generation of algorithms that meet the ART principles. When the aim is to design and implement intelligent agents that are truly capable of providing explanations to people, then we need first to understand the function of explanation in human interaction [92].

5.7 The Ethical Status of AI Systems

Discussing the ethical-reasoning capabilities of AI systems often leads to the discussion of the ethical status of these systems, in particular that of embodied AI systems or robots.

Much of the idea of robot rights derives from the notion of autonomy as an identifying property of AI systems. The term 'autonomy' as understood in philosophy refers to the capacity and right of human persons to decide for themselves, to formulate, think and choose norms, rules and laws that they will follow. That is, it refers to the ability and right to be free to choose one's own goals and purposes in life. The cognitive processes that support and facilitate this are among the ones most closely identified with human dignity and with human agency. Autonomy, in the ethically relevant sense of the word, can only be attributed to living beings who are self-aware, self-conscious, know about the self-authorship of their actions and can think about and explain reasons for their acting against the background of their values and preferences.

It is therefore somewhat of a misnomer to apply the term 'autonomy' to artefacts, however advanced and complex these are. In fact, as stated by Bostrom *"current AI systems have no moral status. We may change, copy, terminate, delete, or use computer programs as we please; at least as far as the programs themselves are concerned. The moral constraints to which we are subject in our dealings with contemporary AI systems, are all grounded in our responsibilities to other beings, such as our fellow humans, not in any duties to the systems themselves."* [21]

The terminology of autonomous systems has gained wide currency in the scientific literature and public debate to refer to the capability of machines to act independently of human direction. However, as discussed in Section 2.3.2, in most cases, this autonomous ability of a machine refers to *operational* or functional 'autonomy'. That is, the ability, given a certain goal or objective, and without direct external intervention, to determine how best to meet this goal, given the system's functionalities and its assessment of the environment. For example, a navigation system can autonomously decide the most suitable route given a destination, and a robotic vacuum cleaning system can calculate the best time and plan to clean your living room. The autonomy for the agent to set its own *goals* or *motives* is not only more complex to realise computationally, but also more controversial and in most cases undesirable. You would not trust your car's navigation system to autonomously set the car's destination, or worse, to determine why you should go to a given place.

In reality, no intelligent artefact – however advanced and sophisticated – should be called 'autonomous' in the original philosophical sense, and therefore it can never be accorded the same form of moral standing as a human being nor inherit human dignity. Human dignity is the core value of liberal democracies, and the foundation of human rights, and seen as an untouchable and unchangeable principle. It implies that meaningful human intervention and participation must be possible in all matters that concern oneself.

However, some scholars and practitioners believe that some 'robot rights' should be considered. There are several interpretations of this concept, which in the popular view mean that intelligent machines, such as robots, would be entitled to some type of rights, in the same way as one considers animal rights. Hollywood and popular authors, in particular often give us scenarios in which robots take, are given or demand rights. This should however stay in the realm of fiction.

In his comprehensive and extensive treatment of the topic of machine rights [69], Gunkel argues that the focus of analysis, where it concerns the role of AI systems, is not about their function ("What can and should AI systems do?") but about the social response to this, i.e. *"How can and should we deal with such systems?"* This observation links to what has been termed system *patiency*, contrasting to the more usual analysis of system *agency*. Any ethical situation has in fact two components: the agent (who initiates and decides on action), and the patient (who is the subject or receiver of that action) [53]. Gunkel links the issue of robot rights to their position of patient in an ethical interaction, and concludes that by inverting the issue, and considering the status of an entity as a result of the ethical treatment it receives, one can achieve a more meaningful discussion of the ethical position of AI systems.

An alternative position is that of Bryson, who argues for a normative discourse rather than a descriptive one, where it concerns the ethical position of AI. In [26], she argues that *"we are unlikely to construct a coherent ethics such that it is ethical to afford AI moral subjectivity. We are therefore obliged not to build AI we are obliged to."* These views are also echoed on the *EPSRC's Principles of Robotics*, which amongst other points, states that *"Robots are manufactured artefacts. They should not be designed in a deceptive way to exploit vulnerable users; instead their machine nature should be transparent"*. These principles declare robots to be artefacts, for which the person responsible should always be clear, because *"Humans, not robots, are responsible agents."* [112]. This position is consistent with that of Responsible AI as described in this book.

5.8 Concluding Remarks

In this section, we discussed the 'can' and the 'ought' of developing systems capable of ethical deliberation. Starting from a naive architecture for such a system, we went on to analyse the requirements and foundations of ethical reasoning, and proposed alternatives for its implementation. In the last section, we discussed the issue of the ethical status of AI systems. As a conclusion, I would like to further elaborate on this last issue.

Currently, much of the discussion around the ethical status of AI or machine rights is anchored in a very anthropomorphic view of the machine, that of an individualised entity, the agent or the patient. It is the area in which people speak of 'the' AI, as being one entity and not a technology area. This, by the way, is also how the classic definition of an autonomous agent puts it: an agent is a "self-contained, concurrently executing software process, that encapsulates some state and is able to communicate with other agents" [75]. However, this view ignores the increasingly distributed and networked nature of AI, composed of a myriad of elements, including people, organisations and AI systems (virtual and embedded), and forming a truly socio-cognitive-technical system.

In this distributed AI reality, we need to be able to analyse the impact components have on each other, the motivations and requirements behind each component, and their contribution to the overall decision. Even in cases where the system is apparently one single entity, it will likely be connected to the Web and therefore be part of a complex, distributed system. For example, self-driving cars are connected to other cars, and receive weather reports through the Web and information about road conditions from sensors on the road. The car itself is nothing more than a cog in the wheel of information and decision-making.

There is therefore an urgent need to study autonomy from the perspective of distribution. Ignoring the need to do so can foster the erosion of responsibility and the inability to handle accountability. Understanding the ethical status of a distributed system is the most important next step in the field of AI ethics.

Finally, as for the question "Can AI systems be ethical?", the answer remains elusive. Building on my experience, I've designed systems that can deliberate between upholding societal norms or rules, and following one's goals. And I have done extensive work on the computational representation and verification of societal aspects of AI systems. Did any of these systems approach true ethical reasoning? Not by far. The systems were never aware that their actions and decision might have any ethical 'flavour' at all. True moral reasoning requires not only being able to make *moral* decisions but to reason about the morality of those decisions. And this requires a huge step ahead.

Investigating a computational theory of ethics will require a formalisation of the concept of responsibility itself, together with clear criteria describing what constitutes an ethical agent, and describing what qualifies as being responsible for something, or having the autonomy to act and understand what that autonomy means. The pursuit of this endeavour will surely contribute to a much more profound understanding of all these notions, and in doing so give us a better understanding of our own ethical reasoning. As such it is, in my opinion, a justifiable scientific endeavour.

5.9 Further Reading

To know more about moral reasoning by AI systems and the different approaches that have been proposed, I recommend:

- WALLACH, W., AND ALLEN, C. *Moral Machines: Teaching Robots Right from Wrong.* Oxford University Press, 2008
- COINTE, N., BONNET, G., AND BOISSIER, O. Ethical judgment of agents' behaviors in multi-agent systems. In *Proceedings of the 2016 International Conference on Autonomous Agents and Multiagent Systems (AAMAS 2016)* (2016), International Foundation for Autonomous Agents and Multiagent Systems, pp. 1106–1114
- CONITZER, V., SINNOTT-ARMSTRONG, W., BORG, J. S., DENG, Y., AND KRAMER, M. Moral decision making frameworks for artificial intelligence. In *Proceedings of the Twenty-Sixth International Joint Conference on Artificial Intelligence (IJCAI 2017)* (2017), pp. 4831–4835
- SERRAMIA, M., LOPEZ-SANCHEZ, M., RODRIGUEZ-AGUILAR, J. A., RODRIGUEZ, M., WOOLDRIDGE, M., MORALES, J., AND ANSOTEGUI, C. Moral values in norm decision making. In *Proceedings of the 17th International Conference on Autonomous Agents and MultiAgent Systems (AAMAS 2018)* (2018), International Foundation for Autonomous Agents and Multiagent Systems, pp. 1294–1302

For further reading on the moral status of AI systems, see:

- GUNKEL, D. J. *Robot Rights.* MIT Press, 2018
- BOSTROM, N., AND YUDKOWSKY, E. The ethics of artificial intelligence. *The Cambridge Handbook of Artificial Intelligence* (2014), 316–334
- BRYSON, J. J. Patiency is not a virtue: the design of intelligent systems and systems of ethics. *Ethics and Information Technology* **20**, 1 (Mar 2018), 15–26
- VAN WYNSBERGHE, A., AND ROBBINS, S. Critiquing the reasons for making artificial moral agents. *Science and Engineering Ethics* (2018), 1–17

Chapter 6
Ensuring Responsible AI in Practice

> "If you can change the world by innovation today so that you can satisfy more of your obligations tomorrow, you have a moral obligation to innovate today."
>
> Jeroen van den Hoven

Where we consider our own responsibility as researchers, developers and users of AI systems, and evaluate the societal instruments needed to ensure responsibility.

6.1 Introduction

In the previous chapters, we have discussed the issue of responsibility with respect to the processes to design, develop, deploy and use AI (Chapter 4), and how to deal with ethical reasoning by the AI systems themselves (Chapter 5). In this chapter, we will look at mechanisms that can ensure that all involved will indeed take the responsible route.

Responsible AI means different things to different people. The concept of Responsible AI also serves as an overall container for many diverse opinions and topics. Depending on the speaker and on the context, it can mean one of the following things:

1. Policies concerning the governance of R&D activities and the deployment and use of AI in societal settings,
2. The role of developers, at individual and collective level,
3. Issues of inclusion, diversity and universal access, and
4. Predictions and reflections on the benefits and risks of AI.

These topics are quite different, as is their impact. Placing all of these issues in the same basket can muddle the discussion, and puts at risk the

© Springer Nature Switzerland AG 2019
V. Dignum, *Responsible Artificial Intelligence*, Artificial Intelligence: Foundations, Theory, and Algorithms, https://doi.org/10.1007/978-3-030-30371-6_6

achievement of constructive solutions to each of the topics. It can also contribute to increase the fear of AI from the general public and with it the risk of the proliferation of ungrounded, dystopic views about what AI is.

The most urgent of these topics is perhaps the first one. AI systems use data that we generate in our daily lives, and are as such a mirror of our interests, weaknesses and differences. AI, like any other technology, is not value-neutral. Understanding the values behind the technology and deciding on how we want our values to be incorporated in AI systems requires that we are also able to decide on what we want AI to mean in our societies. It implies deciding on ethical guidelines, governance policies, incentives and regulations. It implies that we are aware of differences in interests and aims behind AI systems developed by others, according to other cultures and principles. An extension, or alternative, to regulation is certification. Certification is a means of risk regulation and quality assurance that ensures that the products or services they certify meet criteria specified by professional associations, standards organisations or government agencies. We discuss the issues of regulation and certification in Section 6.2.

As for the second topic, it is important to realise that AI does not just materialise. We make it happen. Researchers and developers of AI systems for a large part determine how those systems will behave and what kind of capabilities they will exhibit. Many professions are bound by codes of conduct outlining the proper practices for those professions. The International Federation of Accountants defines a code of conduct as being the *"principles, values, standards, or rules of behaviour that guide the decisions, procedures and systems of an organisation in a way that (a) contributes to the welfare of its key stakeholders, and (b) respects the rights of all constituents affected by its operations."*[1] In fact, society expects strict codes of conduct from those professions it depends on, including health professionals, military, accountants and many others. Given the role of software engineers in the AI systems and applications that shape our world, it is probably time to expect some standards of conduct from this professional group. We will further discuss this issue in Section 6.3.

On the issue of inclusion, diversity and access to AI much has been said and written, in particular relating to bias (cf. Section 4.3.3 for more on bias). However, these issues are also relevant for the environments where AI is developed, and have a strong link to education. Inclusion is a necessary condition for diversity in development teams and AI professionals. This requires more than metrics on demographics; it is important to understand how inclusion is experienced. Broadening engineering education curricula to include the humanities and social sciences that are essential to ensure the responsible design and development of AI will also contribute to a more diverse student population. We further discuss this issue in Section 6.4.

---

[1]   https://www.ifac.org/publications-resources/defining-and-developing-effective-code-conduct-organizations

On the other hand, the media has given disproportionate attention to the last topic. Dystopic views of a future dominated by our robotic overlords seem to sell well and are backed by some scholars (typically from other disciplines), and a disproportionate number of tech-billionaires. However, as Luciano Floridi remarks, even if such a future is logically possible it is utterly unlikely, and focus on these issues is actually a distraction from the real problems that are already affecting us [54]. Even though the topic has fascinated people for ages, the main risk here is that focusing on possible future risks is basically a distraction from the very real risks that we are facing already: privacy and security, consequences for human labour, algorithmic bias, just to cite a few. We will further discuss the issue of the AI narrative in Section 6.5.

6.2 Governance for Responsible AI

In recent years, we have seen a rise of efforts around the ethical, societal and legal impact of AI. These are the result of concerted action by national and transnational governance bodies, including the European Union, the OECD, the UK, France, Canada and others, but have also originated from bottom-up initiatives, launched by practitioners and the scientific community. A few of the most well-known initiatives are:

- the IEEE initiative on Ethics of Autonomous and Intelligent Systems[2]
- the High Level Expert Group on AI of the European Commission[3]
- the Partnership on AI[4]
- the French AI for Humanity strategy[5]
- the Select Committee on AI of the British House of Lords[6]

These initiatives aim at providing concrete recommendations, standards and policy suggestions to support the development, deployment and use of AI systems. Other initiatives have focused on analysing the values and principles to which AI systems and the development thereof should adhere. Examples of such lists are

- the Asilomar principles[7]
- the Barcelona declaration[8]

---

[2] https://ethicsinaction.ieee.org/
[3]   https://ec.europa.eu/digital-single-market/en/high-level-expert-group-artificial-intelligence
[4] https://www.partnershiponai.org/
[5] https://www.aiforhumanity.fr/en/
[6] https://www.parliament.uk/ai-committee
[7] https://futureoflife.org/ai-principles/
[8] https://www.iiia.csic.es/barcelonadeclaration/

- the Montreal declaration[9]
- the ethical guidelines of the Japanese Society for Artificial Intelligence.[10]

Analysing these different lists of principles and values it is clear that all the initiatives make human well-being central to AI development and most recognise in general the ethical principles of Accountability and Responsibility. The initiatives further focus on different types of principles, which can be grouped into three main classes: Societal, Legal and Technical. Allowing for the use of synonyms or slightly different terminologies, the main issues identified are depicted in Figure 6.1.

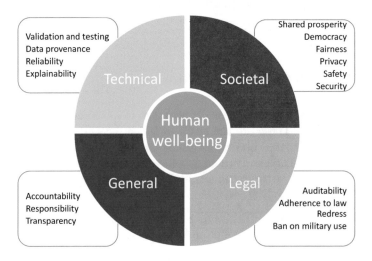

Figure 6.1: The main values and ethical principles identified by the different initiatives

There is also a set of initiatives that focuses on the specific issues of ethics for robotics, in the tradition of the classic Asimov's Laws:

- the EPSRC Principles of robotics[11]
- the Foundation for Responsible Robotics.[12]

In fact, hardly a week goes by without news about yet another declaration of principles for AI, or of other initiatives at national or corporate level. For up-to-date information on all such initiatives check Alan Winfield's blog [13] and the crowdsourced effort coordinated by Doteveryone.[14]

---

[9]   https://nouvelles.umontreal.ca/en/article/2017/11/03/montreal-declaration-for-a-responsible-development-of-artificial-intelligence/

[10] http://ai-elsi.org/wp-content/uploads/2017/05/JSAI-Ethical-Guidelines-1.pdf

[11] See [16]

[12] http://responsiblerobotics.org/

[13] http://alanwinfield.blogspot.com/2017/12

[14] https://goo.gl/ibffk4 (maintained in Google docs)

Ensuring responsible AI is however more than setting up lists of desired principles, standards or recommendations. It requires action. Possible mechanisms for this action are regulation, certification and codes of conduct. These will be discussed further in Section 6.3.

6.2.1 Regulation

Whenever regulation is mentioned with respect to AI development and use, usually one of two issues is mentioned. Firstly, the fear that regulation will stifle innovation and progress. Secondly, the issue of whether current laws and regulations are at all sufficient to deal with the complexities of AI. In my opinion, both are too short-sighted.

Given the dynamic nature of AI, we cannot wait for regulation until the technology is mature. Already now AI is impacting individuals and society, changing cognitive and interaction functions and impacting our well-being. However, as we have seen in previous chapters, there is no established definition of what AI is, and without this it is very difficult to determine what should be the focus of regulation. Moreover, as has been observed by the panel that produced the 100 Years Study on AI Report [116], the risks and considerations are too different in different domains to enable a generic regulatory approach. This means that rather than regulating AI itself, regulating its use in specific areas such as healthcare or the military provides more suitable instruments to ensure its proper application and can better be inserted into existing regulatory forms.

Furthermore, it is important to realise that not all regulation is negative. This is specifically the case when regulation takes the form of incentives or investment programs that nudge organisations to pursue a specific type of applications or technological approaches.

As for the issue of the suitability of current regulations, it should be clear that AI is an artefact. As such, much of product and service liability laws applies to its use. There is however the need for close collaboration between legal and AI experts to collaborate on the evaluation and possible update of existing laws to specific cases of AI applications.

Finally, regulation can also be seen as a means to further scientific development of AI. For example, consider the case in which legislation will restrict use of data and demand explanation of all results achieved by an AI system. These requirements probably mean that many of the current approaches, based on neural networks and deep learning, are not able to meet these demands. This can be seen as a limitation on the use of AI and be approached with complaints and refusal to comply, claiming economic losses and delays to development. But it can also be seen as a challenge to be taken. Then researchers need to go back to the drawing board to come up with novel learning and reasoning techniques that do ensure explainability and sustainable use of data without compromising efficiency.

AI is by far not done yet. Current machine learning techniques are just an intermediate step on the path of progress. If regulation is the means to further this progress, then we had better embrace it. Such an approach does require a culture of openness and cooperation between scientists, developers, policymakers and ethicists in order to ensure that regulations create the incentives to development that benefit both technology development and society. It is encouraging to see that the need for dialogue between different parties is increasingly being acknowledged by all.

6.2.2 Certification

How do you know that the eggs you bought yesterday are in fact organic and free-range? All eggs look the same to me... However, I tend to trust the certification stamps that indicate that free-range eggs have been evaluated along a set of metrics that defines what a free-range egg is. If I were so inclined, it would be possible to assess these rules and who are the certification authorities.[15] The point here is of course not the eggs, but the process. Even though I don't know much about eggs, I still feel sufficiently informed and empowered in order to make the decision about which eggs to buy.

We can consider similar mechanisms for AI systems. In this case, independent and trusted institutions would validate and test algorithms, applications and products against a set of well-defined principles (possibly derived from the recommendations described above) and guarantee the quality of the system. We, as users of such systems, would then have the choice of what type of system would best meet our own personal requirements.

Such a certification approach can be combined with a regulatory one. In this case, regulation would specify the minimum set of principles and their interpretation that must hold for all systems in a given country or region, similar to the data protection regulations in force within the European Union.[16] Beyond the minimum requirements laid down by regulation, certification supports business differentiation at the same time it ensures consumer protection.

Currently, several initiatives towards AI ethical certification are being launched, including by the IEEE. The IEEE's Ethics Certification Program for Autonomous and Intelligent Systems (ECPAIS) aims to create specifications for certifying and marking processes that advance transparency and accountability, and reduce algorithmic bias in AI Systems.

---

[15] If you really are interested in eggs, check for instance Wikipedia's information concerning US, EU and Australia: https://en.wikipedia.org/wiki/Free-range_eggs

[16] Cf. https://eugdpr.org/.

In our recent White Paper proposing an ethical framework for AI, we have advised the creation of a new EU oversight agency responsible for the protection of public welfare through the scientific evaluation and supervision of AI products, software, systems and services, with similar aims [56]. At the same time, several commercial organisations, including Accenture and PwC, are announcing auditing services for the analysis of algorithms.

6.3 Codes of Conduct

Another way to ensure responsibility for AI systems is the development of self-regulatory codes of conduct for professionals working in data- and AI-related fields, describing specific ethical duties related to the impact of the systems being developed. This approach follows similar lines to other critical and socially sensitive professions, such as medical doctors or lawyers. Such a code of conduct can serve as a differentiating factor, but as it gets more common, also as a requirement imposed on those who conduct AI-related activities. As with certification, when more people understand the merits of a responsible approach to AI, we can expect that adherence to codes of conduct will be demanded from developers and providers [56].

A professional code of conduct is a public statement developed for and by a professional group to

- reflect shared principles about practice, conduct and ethics of those exercising the profession,
- describe the quality of behaviour that reflects the expectations of the profession and the community,
- provide a clear statement to society about these expectations, and
- enable professionals to reflect on their own ethical decisions.

A code of conduct supports professionals to assess and resolve difficult professional and ethical dilemmas. While in the case of ethical dilemmas there is no correct solution, the professionals can give account of their actions by referring to the code.

Many organisations and enterprises have their own codes of conduct. Even if in many cases adherence to the code is voluntary, there are professions which require allegiance to their code. This is the case of professional orders, or guilds, in many countries, where membership is a necessary condition for the practice of the profession. The most well known is the Hippocratic Oath or Physician's Pledge (the Declaration of Geneva) taken by medical doctors.

Just recently ACM, the Association for Computing Machinery, the largest international association of computing professionals, updated their code of conduct [65]. This voluntary code is *"a collection of principles and guidelines designed to help computing professionals make ethically responsible decisions in professional practice. It translates broad ethical principles into concrete statements about professional conduct*.[17] This code explicitly addresses issues associated with the development of AI systems, namely issues of emergent properties, discrimination and privacy. Specifically, it calls out the responsibility of technologists to ensure that systems are inclusive and accessible to all, and requires that they are knowledgeable about privacy issues.

6.4 Inclusion and Diversity

Inclusion and diversity are a broader societal challenge and central to AI development. Research and development of AI systems must be informed by diversity, in all the meaning of diversity, and obviously including gender, cultural background and ethnicity. But there is also growing evidence that cognitive diversity contributes to better decision-making. Therefore development teams should include social scientists, philosophers and others, as well as ensuring gender, ethnicity and cultural differences. It is important to diversify the AI development workforce, along all pertinent dimensions [56]. Regulation and codes of conduct can specify targets and goals, along with incentives, as a way to foster diversity in AI teams.

It is equally important to diversify the expertise of those working on AI. In order to understand the ethical, social, legal and economic impact of AI and evaluate how design decisions contribute to this impact, AI professionals need to have basic knowledge of philosophy, social science, law and economics.

Education plays an important role here. AI is no longer an engineering discipline. In fact, AI is too important to be left to engineers alone! AI is really transdisciplinary. Most current AI and Robotics curricula worldwide deliver engineers with a too-narrow task view. The wide impact of AI on society requires a broadening of engineering education to include, at least, the following aspects:

- analysis of the distributed nature of AI applications as these integrate socio-technical systems, and the complexity of human-agent interaction;
- reflection on the meaning and global effect of the autonomous, emergent, decentralised, self-organising character of distributed learning entities;
- incremental design and development frameworks, and the unforeseen positive and negative influence of individual decisions at system level, and how these impact human rights, democracy and education;
- the consequences of inclusion and diversity in design, and how these inform processes and results;
- understanding of governance and normative issues: not only in terms of competences and responsibilities, but also terms of health, safety, risks, explanations and accountability;

---

[17] https://www.acm.org/articles/bulletins/2018/july/new-code-of-ethics-released

- understanding of the underlying societal, legal and economic models of socio-technical systems;
- knowledge of value-based design approaches and of ethical frameworks.

Broadening AI curricula is possibly also a way to attract a more diverse student population. When AI curricula are known to be transdisciplinary, it can be expected that female students, who traditionally (at least in Western societies) tend to choose humanities and social subjects over engineering ones, may be motivated to choose AI. In parallel, other curricula need to include subjects on the theory and practice of AI. For example, law curricula need to prepare law experts to address legal and regulatory issues around AI.

Finally, it is important to realise that besides human diversity, it is also important to consider cultural diversity, which includes factors such as education, religion and language. AI is increasingly pervasive and applied across cultures and regions. Failure to understand cultural diversity impacts negatively the universal right to access to the advantages that the technology brings about. In an increasingly connected AI world, incentives and regulations can support awareness of and commitment to a diverse perspective, ensuring that AI applications are truly adaptable to a diverse cultural space, and thus enabling access to all.

6.5 The AI Narrative

Responsibility in AI begins with a proper AI narrative, which demystifies the possibilities and the processes of AI technologies and enables all to be able to participate in the discussion of the role of AI in society.

Since its origins, the AI field has gone through ups and downs, winters and periods of hype. However, never before we have witnessed the current level of excitement (and fear) by so many, in so many areas. AI is breaking through in many different application domains, with results that impress even the most knowledgeable experts. Three main factors are leading this development: the increasing availability of large amounts of data, improved algorithms, and substantial computational power. However, of these three only the improvement of algorithms can rightfully be seen as a contribution from the AI field. The other two are fortunate contingencies.

The awareness that AI has the potential to impact our lives and our world as no other technology has done before is rightfully raising many questions concerning its ethical, legal, societal and economic effects. Currently, hardly a day goes by without the introduction of a new declaration or set of guidelines concerning the impact of AI and how to deal with it. Governments, corporations and social organisations alike are coming forward with proposals and declarations of their commitment to an accountable, responsible, transparent approach to AI, where human values and ethical principles are leading. This

is a much-needed development, one to which I've dedicated my research in
the last few years.

AI is not magic. Contrary to what some may want us to believe, the algorithms used by AI are not a magic wand that gives their users powers of
omniscience or the ability to achieve any and everything. AI uses algorithms,
but then so does any other computer program or engineering process. Algorithms are far from magic and have been around for thousands of years. [18]
In fact, the easiest definition of algorithm is that of a recipe, a set of precise
rules to achieve a certain result. Every time you add two numbers, you are
using an algorithm. When you bake an apple pie you are also following an
algorithm, a recipe. By itself, a recipe has never turned into an apple pie.
The end result of your pie has more to do with your baking skills and your
choice of ingredients. The same applies to AI algorithms: for a large part the
result depends on the input data, and on the ability of those who trained it.
And, in the same way as we have the choice to use organic apples to make
our pie, in AI we also have the choice to use data that respects and ensures
fairness, privacy, transparency and all other values we hold dear. This is what
Responsible AI is about, the decisions taken concerning the scope, the rules
and the resources that are used to develop, deploy and use AI systems. AI is
not just the algorithm, or the data that it uses. It is a complex combination
of decisions, opportunities and resources.

A proper AI narrative is also about the perceived need to understand the
benefits, and potential dangers, of the use of anthropomorphic representations of AI. From Sophia the robot addressing the United Nations council,
to Google's chatbot booking hairdresser's appointments, AI systems are increasingly impersonating humans, with different levels of success. Whereas
in many cases, it may be necessary that AI systems do interact in ways that
are indistinguishable from people, concerns about misleading and the setting
of unrealistic expectations cannot be ignored.

While the significance of these platforms for experimentation and explo-
ration in robotics, AI and human-robot experimentation cannot be ignored,
it is as important to determine how to ensure that users and the public in
general are not deceived by them. In their current forms, these platforms are
not even close to what can be considered human-level AI. Yes, they can trick
the hairdresser into believing that it is a real person making the appointment
in the case of Google Duplex.[19] or the public at an event into believing that
it really has emotions, in the case of Sophia the robot.[20] But none would pass

---

[18] The word algorithm derives from al-Kwarizmi 'the man of Warizm' (now Khiva), the
name given to the ninth-century mathematician Abu Ja'far Muhammad ibn Musa, author
of widely translated works on algebra and arithmetic.

[19]   See   https://ai.googleblog.com/2018/05/duplex-ai-system-for-natural-
conversation.html for details.

[20] Check http://goertzel.org/sophias-ai-some-comments/ for a description of how
Sophia works.

the Turing test nor be able to reply to questions outside their predetermined scope.

Human-level intelligence and behaviour are obviously aims of AI research, in order to be able to support and empower people in their tasks, but also to achieve a better understanding of what is intelligence. In addition, in the future robots and other AI platforms will play an increasingly important role in the future, in our homes, in our work, and as means to increase and support the quality of our interactions. An important area of research is to understand how human-agent and human-robot interactions will affect our own understanding of these systems and how we will interact with them. Responsible AI in this area means that, the use of human-like properties (voice, appearance, etc.) must meet a strict ethical evaluation of the purpose and implementation, ensuring the participation of users and other stakeholders in the design, and that they are given sufficient alternatives to be able to judge the necessity for the anthropomorphic properties.

6.6 Concluding Remarks

Increasingly, AI systems will be taking decisions that affect our lives, in smaller or larger ways. In all areas of application, AI must be able to take into account societal values, moral and ethical considerations and weigh the respective priorities of values held by different stakeholders and in multicultural contexts, explain its reasoning, and guarantee transparency. As the capabilities for autonomous decision-making grow, perhaps the most important issue to consider is the need to rethink responsibility. Being fundamentally tools, AI systems are fully under the control and responsibility of their owners or users. However, their potential autonomy and capability to learn require that their design considers accountability, responsibility and transparency principles in an explicit and systematic manner. The development of AI algorithms has so far been led by the goal of improving performance, leading to opaque black boxes. Putting human values at the core of AI systems calls for a mind-shift of researchers and developers towards the goal of improving transparency rather than performance, which will lead to novel and exciting techniques and applications.

Some researchers claim that given that AI systems are artefacts, the discussion of the ethics of AI is somewhat misplaced. Indeed, we, people, are the ones responsible for these systems. We, people, are the ones determining the questions that AI systems can answer and how to deal with the results of their decisions and actions. The main concern of Responsible AI is thus the identification of the relative responsibility of all actors involved in the design, development, deployment and use of AI systems.

In order to design AI systems that are sensitive to moral principles and human values, methods for Responsible AI rest on three pillars of equal importance. Firstly, society must be prepared to take responsibility for AI's impact. This means that researchers and developers should be trained to be aware of their own responsibility where it concerns the development of AI systems with direct impact in society. This requires extra efforts in developing and delivering education and training materials, and the development of codes of conduct for AI developers. This in turn requires methods and tools to understand and integrate moral, societal and legal values with technological developments in AI.

This means that Responsible AI is firstly an issue of governance. It is up to governments and citizens to determine how issues of liability should be regulated. For example, who will be to blame if a self-driving car harms a pedestrian? The builder of the hardware (e.g. of the sensors used by the car to perceive the environment)? The builder of the software that enables the car to decide on a path? The authorities that allow the car on the road? The owner that personalised the car's decision-making settings to meet her preferences? And how can current product liability laws be understood in the face of systems that act as a result of a long (autonomous) learning process? All these questions, and more, must inform the regulations that societies put in place towards responsible use of AI systems.

Secondly, Responsible AI implies the need for mechanisms that enable AI systems to act according to ethics and human values. Whether we design them in that way or not, AI systems will make and are already making decisions that we would consider to have an ethical flavour if they were made by people. Being aware of this is what responsible AI is all about. How do we design systems that take implicitly 'ethical' decisions? Or how do we design the system to ensure that it refers the decision to someone to take because it is an ethical decision? And where is the border between decisions that are not ethical and ones that are? This requires models and algorithms to represent and reason about, and take decisions based on, human values, and to justify their decisions according to their effect on those values. Current (deep learning) mechanisms are unable to meaningfully link decisions to inputs, and therefore cannot explain their acts in ways that we can understand.

Last but certainly not least, Responsible AI is about participation. It is necessary to understand how different people work with and live with AI technologies across cultures in order to develop frameworks for Responsible AI. In fact, AI does not stand in itself, but must be understood as part of sociotechnical relations, with all their diversity. Here again education plays an important role, to ensure that knowledge of the potential of AI is widespread, to make people aware that they can participate in shaping its societal development, and as a basis to ensure diversity and inclusion. A new and more ambitious form of governance is one of the most pressing needs in order to ensure that inevitable AI advances will be accessible to all, and serve societal good.

6.7 Further Reading

Links to many of the current initiatives around AI policy have already been provided in this chapter. I advise you to consult those links and references for more information.

There is also a growing number of national and corporate initiatives on Responsible AI, most resulting in manifestos or lists of principles to be upheld by the initiator. A good overview of national initiatives is the one maintained by Tim Dutton: `https://medium.com/politics-ai/an-overview-of-national-ai-strategies-2a70ec6edfd`.

Chapter 7
Looking Further

> "Watch out for arguments about
> future technology that is magical."
>
> Rodney Brooks

Where we look at the societal impact of AI now and in the not too far future, considering, in particular, the future of jobs and education, and the potential risks associated with AI and the possibility of super-intelligence.

7.1 Introduction

In his article "Seven Deadly Sins of AI Predictions",[1] Rodney Brooks quotes Amara's Law: *"We tend to overestimate the effect of a technology in the short run and underestimate the effect in the long run."* In its relatively short history, AI has been overestimated several times, in the 1960s, in the 1980s, leading to the so-called, AI winters, and underestimated at least as many times. I've been working on AI since the late 1980s and during most of my working life I have needed to justify why was I doing research in such an esoteric field, unlikely to ever produce any useful product. But the current developments in AI and machine learning would not have been possible without the work laid out in those cold winter years.

Nevertheless, today's media and business interest would almost make one believe that AI is a new technology which 'suddenly' has taken over the world. The current rise of AI is often compared to the Industrial Revolution. In 2017, Steven Cave, executive director of the Leverhulme Centre for the Future of Intelligence, referred to the AI revolution as "...likely to happen even faster

---

[1] See https://www.technologyreview.com/s/609048/the-seven-deadly-sins-of-ai-predictions/.

© Springer Nature Switzerland AG 2019
V. Dignum, *Responsible Artificial Intelligence*, Artificial Intelligence: Foundations, Theory, and Algorithms, https://doi.org/10.1007/978-3-030-30371-6_7

– so the potential damage is even greater."[2] The pace may be increasing, but actually, humankind has always been concerned with the pace of technological change.

Moreover, machines have been making decisions for us for quite some time, and are doing it autonomously in many cases. My thermostat decides whether to turn the central heating on or off based on the information it has about my preferred room temperature; the electronic gate in my local train station decides whether to grant me access to the platforms based on the information it gets on my travel credit and on constraints given to it by the local travel authorities; Google decides which of the trillions of Web pages I am more likely to want to see when I search for something; and Netflix tells me what I might want to watch tonight, based on the information it has about my preferences and those of people it thinks are similar to me.

What makes AI decision-making different, and for some people more worrisome, is the opacity of those decisions, and the perceived lack of control over the actions that AI systems take based on those decisions. This view is both stifling and dismissive. Stifling because it may lead to a feeling of powerlessness in our control over machines, and dismissive because it may lead humans to feel less responsibility for the use and outcomes of AI systems.

As we have seen throughout this book, we, humans, are the ones that determine the optimisation goals and the utility functions at the basis of machine learning algorithms; we are the ones that decide what the machine should be maximising. Indeed, even in the famous *paperclip maximiser* example by Nick Bostrom [20], someone once gave this maximisation goal to the unfortunate intelligent factory.

AI does potentially pose many risks and can be used for evil by evildoers. However, AI also brings enormous potential to improve the lives of many, and to ensure human rights for all. It is up to us to decide:

- Are we building algorithms to maximise shareholder profit or to maximise fair distribution of resources in a community? For example, algorithms that can provide solutions to tragedy-of-the-commons situations and support fair distribution of resources;
- Are we using AI to optimise company performance or to optimise crop yield for small farmers around the world? For example, AI systems that provide real-time information on fertiliser levels, planting and harvesting moments and weather conditions;
- Are we building AI systems to emulate and replace people, misleading users about their machine nature, or are we building AI to ensure well-being, participation and inclusion? For example, translation services to improve cross-cultural communication, tools to provide access to information and education for all, and that curb the distribution of fake news.

---

[2] See https://www.telegraph.co.uk/business/leaders-of-transformation/horizons/intelligence-revolution/

It is up to us to decide. AI development can be motivated by money and shareholder value, or by human rights and well-being, and societal values. It is up to us to decide. Is AI going to enhance our facilities and enable us to work better, or is it going to replace us? The impact of AI on jobs is perhaps one of the most-discussed aspects of the potential technological advance that AI brings. We will discuss this issue in Section 7.2.1.

The power of decision is the power of all of us. Researchers, developers, policymakers, users. Every one of us.

But to use this power we need to be informed and involved in the policy and strategy discussions around AI. All of us. In the same way that war is too important to be left to the generals, and democracy is too important to be left to the politicians, AI is too important to be left to the technocrats. This implies that we need a multidisciplinary approach to AI, but most of all that we need a different approach to education that enables all to be involved. We discussed the importance of education with respect to inclusion and diversity in Section 6.4, and will reflect on the consequences of AI for education in Section 7.2.2.

We need also to consider the risks associated with AI technology. These can be either intended or unintended but in both cases may lead to profound negative consequences. We will discuss the main risks in Section 7.2.3. In Section 7.2.4 we reflect on the many beneficial uses of AI, the field of AI for Good.

Finally, a book about AI cannot be complete without some reflection on the possibility and plausibility of super-intelligence. We will look at this in Section 7.3.

7.2 AI and Society

As Artificial Intelligence technology becomes better at many tasks that have so far been done by people, we can expect to see an increase in efficiency and wealth. However, many concerns have been voiced as to how these benefits are going to be guaranteed and shared by the whole of humankind and not remain the privilege of a few. Concerns about the impact of Artificial Intelligence on society as we know it, are currently widely voiced by experts, media and policymakers alike. These concerns mostly follow two main directions. On the one hand, worries about the impact of AI on our current society: the number and nature of jobs, privacy, (cyber)security and deployment of autonomous weapons are some of the most-cited issues. On the other hand, the possible existential risks associated with super-intelligence, or singularity, that is, the dangers for humankind in the event that AI systems surpass human intelligence.

It is an often-heard claim that Artificial Intelligence has the potential to disrupt all areas of society and business. Many initiatives, news reports and projects are concerned with the societal impact of AI and the means to ensure that this impact is a positive one.

7.2.1 Future of Jobs

AI's impact may be be most noticeable on how jobs and work will look in the not too far future. When AI systems will replace people in many traditional jobs, we must rethink the meaning of work. Jobs will change but more importantly the character of jobs will change. Meaningful occupations are those who contribute to the welfare of society, the fulfilment of oneself and the advance of mankind. These are not necessarily equated with our current understanding of 'paid jobs'. Used well, AI systems can free us to care for each other, engage in arts, hobbies and sports, enjoy nature, and meditate, i.e. those things that give us energy and make us happy. But used without concern for societal impact and human well-being, AI can lead to massive job losses, increased inequality, and social unrest. Defining proper incentives and rewards to ensure well-being and sustainability, and a new definition of wealth and meaningful occupation are needed to ensure that AI is used for the good of humanity and the environment. In parallel, many new jobs will appear for which skilled human workers are needed with a set of skills that combine technical education with the humanities, arts and social sciences.

AI will perform hard, dangerous or boring work for us; it will help us to save lives and cope with disasters; and it will entertain us and make our daily life more comfortable. In fact, current AI systems are already changing our daily lives, almost entirely in ways that improve human health, safety and productivity. In the coming years we can expect AI systems to be increasingly be used in domains such as transportation, service robots, healthcare, education, low-resource communities, public safety and security, employment and the workplace, and entertainment. These systems must be introduced in ways that build trust and understanding, respect human and civil rights, and are in line with cultural and social context.

It is urgent to anticipate and prepare for the impact of our digital future. Next to the imperative technological skills, increasingly the human workforce of the future will be challenged to cooperate, adapt to an ever-changing world, and maintain a questioning mind. AI applications will be participating in the digital ecosystem alongside us, and whereas these systems can help us in many ways, co-existing alongside AI systems will necessarily bring with it changes in the way we, people, interact, learn and work.

In general, experts believe that AI technology is both creating and destroying jobs, and notably also that it's unlikely to cause a major reduction in the number of jobs in the future. We know from historical trends that in the long term, technological advances have always been beneficial for the quality and quantity of jobs. However, in the short term, disruptions can be expected to specific occupations and specific demographic groups. Studies also show that regions where job opportunities are diverse will likely adjust better to change [59].

Education and training are mandatory to ensure that disruptions are minimised. Even though we cannot know for sure which jobs will exist in the future, it is expected that human skills of empathy, caring, creativity and ease to quickly adapt to unforeseen situations will be central. Also, the demand for skills that combine technical education with the humanities, arts and social sciences is likely to increase. We also need to foster the use of AI to support the development of new skills that will enable people to adapt to new types of jobs [56].

There is also an important role for regulation here to ensure that the burden of change is balanced across regions, demographic groups and job areas. Possible regulatory interventions that are currently being considered include taxation (e.g. the infamous robot tax[3]) and 'universal basic income' schemes. This also requires social partners, such as trade unions and professional organisations to be involved in the conversation and to take their own responsibility for the impact of AI.

In conclusion, technological developments in the last century led to mass production and mass consumption. Until very recently, having has been the main goal and competition the main drive: 'I am what I have'. Digital developments, including AI, favour openness over competition: open data, open source and open access. The drive is now quickly shifting to sharing: 'I am what I share'. Combined with the changing role of work, this novel view of wealth requires a new view of economy and finance, but can contribute to a fundamental positive change to society.

7.2.2 Future of Education

The digital transformation of society is possibly the main challenge of this century. By the end of 2013, those that have grown up in a digital world started to outnumber those that had to adapt to it. However, capacity building to ensure that everybody is able to contribute to the digital ecosystem and to fully participate in the workforce is lagging behind, and current education curricula are perhaps not the most suitable to meet the demands of future work.

Considering that *"the tools that we shape, will thereafter shape us"*,[4] the digital ecosystem will bring along a redefinition of fundamental human values, including our current understanding of work and wealth. In order to ensure the skills needed for resilient and sustainable capacity building for the digital

---

[3] See https://www.techemergence.com/robot-tax-summary-arguments/ for a summary of the main arguments for and against robot taxation.

[4] Quote attributed to media theorist Marshall McLuhan.

ecosystem, the following aspects must be central in education curricula across the world:

- **Collaborate**: The digital ecosystem makes possible and assumes collaboration across distance, time, cultures and contexts. The world is indeed a village, and all of us are the inhabitants of this village. Skills are needed to interact, build relationships and show the self-awareness needed to work effectively with others in person and virtually, across cultures.
- **Question**: AI systems are great at finding answers, and will do this increasingly well. It is up to us to ask the right questions, and to critically evaluate results in order to be able to contribute to responsible implementation of solutions.
- **Imagine**: Skills to approach problem-solving creatively, using empathy, logic and novel thinking, are needed. For this, humanities education is paramount and should be included in all technology curricula.
- **Learn to learn**: The ability to adapt and pick up new skills quickly is vital for success, requiring us to continuously learn and grow, and adapt to change. Being able to understand what it is necessary to know, and knowing when to apply a particular concept as well as knowing how to do it, are key to continuous success.

The digital age is a time for reinvention and creativity. Capacity building must embrace these skills alongside technological expertise. This shows that the traditional separation between humanities, arts, social sciences and STEM (Science, Technology, Engineering and Mathematics) is not suitable for the needs of the digital age. More than multidisciplinary, future students need to be transdisciplinary: creating a unity of intellectual frameworks beyond the disciplinary perspectives. In fact, I would say that Artificial Intelligence is not a STEM discipline. It is in essence trans-disciplinary and requires a spectrum of capabilities that is not covered by current education curricula. It is urgent to redesign studies. This also gives a unique opportunity to truly achieve inclusion and diversity across academic fields.

7.2.3 Dealing with Risks

AI brings in itself enormous potential to improve the lives of many, and to ensure human rights for all. It is for all our sakes that we should ensure that risks are minimised. As discussed in Chapter 6, a combination of regulation, certification, education and self-awareness are important towards this endeavour.

Whether risks are intended or unintended, they can have profound consequences for safety, democracy and the very meaning of being human. In the following, we discuss some of these issues. Note that this discussion aims at presenting an overall idea and does not pretend to be an exhaustive list of all potential risks.

Dealing with risk requires that people are equipped with the competencies to control the systems they interact with, rather than be controlled by them. This again requires education and the willingness of societal institutions to take responsibility for the ways we are allowing AI to shape society.

Safety

Ensuring that AI systems are safe, is a main condition for trust.

Safety is about being sure that the system will indeed do what it is supposed to do, without harming users, resources or the environment. Also it is about knowing that the purpose of the system is beneficial and according to human rights and values.

Unintended consequences are of many sorts. They can be errors in programming, but also incorrect application of resources, regulations or algorithms. Biased results, breaches of privacy, or erroneous decisions are some of the results. As we have discussed in Chapter 4 a structured, open and value-centred design process is of utmost importance to mitigate and correct unintended risks. Moreover, formal mechanisms are needed to measure and direct the adaptability of AI systems and to ensure robust processes. Safeguards that enable fall-back plans in case of problems with the AI system are also necessary. In some cases this can mean that the AI system switches from statistical to rule-based procedures; in other cases it can mean that the system will request an human operator to take over control.

Worse is the case of intended malicious uses of AI. These range from minor nuisances such as email spam, to full-fledged cyber warfare [117]. A recent report [24] surveys the landscape of potential security threats from malicious uses of artificial intelligence technologies, and proposes ways to better forecast, prevent and mitigate these threats. The report recommends a combination of regulation and taking responsibility to address this issue. In particular, researchers and developers are urged to consider carefully the dual-use purpose of their work. Moreover, developing AI techniques that are able to assess and deflect malicious objectives of other AI systems can also contribute to minimise the effects of misuse of AI.

Democracy

It is increasingly clear that AI will contribute to a fundamental change in the way in which we organise the economy and society. But is AI the end of democracy as we know it, as some have predicted [72]? The current ideal of democracy is grounded on the individual's right to self-determination [32].

By affecting people's self-determination, AI is potentially affecting the democratic process, for better or for worse.

What we are currently seeing is that the capability to even out majority sentiment, traditionally a function of democratic institutions, is eroding under the possibilities of AI systems. Increasingly, the Internet has rendered the diversity of citizens' views more salient, and has proven a powerful medium for discontented citizens to put pressure on democratic institutions and force changes in policies. At the same time, manipulating public sentiment towards specific standpoints is made easy by (fake) news targeted at individual sentiments and preferences. The political risks associated with AI refer to the risks of imbalance of power between individuals, groups or values in society, and are made possible by the increased power and speed in collection and processing of information.

Often democracy is taken as given. The current view is that democracy is the great equaliser, something that we need and want to uphold in all cases. However, critical perspectives on democracy show that traditional democracy often privileges a specific kind of individual/citizen as well as rules out more radical notions of democracy.

On the other hand, AI and digital technologies are already disrupting the traditional view of democracy, and not always for the better, ensuring that processes are more inclusive. In fact, if anything, AI is strengthening the link between democracy and economics, supporting the manipulation of information to meet the needs of a few, and enabling the emergence of super economic powers that are outside democratic scrutiny and control. When algorithms are used to decide our access to information about a news item, a political candidate or a business, opinions and votes can shift, and potential government's be made or broken. Because algorithmic censorship is mostly unregulated, large corporations can in principle decide what information we have, outside the traditional democratic processes of governance and accountability. Moreover, these same corporations also own most of our, and our governments, data, by the conditions under which we use their products to share, store and manage information.

Thus, democracy as we know it is changing its forms. It is an open area of research to investigate how democracy is changing through the use and effect of AI.

Another important issue is that of participation and control. AI systems currently are for a large part owned and dominated by large, private corporations, which not only determine how and what AI is being designed and deployed but also control and formally own all the data shared through those systems. As such these corporations have a huge impact on how we create and design our public space, 'the commons' that we use, and that are also used by municipalities, schools, etc. for communicating with citizens, pupils and parents.

In short, the ones that control AI can *de facto* control democratic processes and institutions. Without clear regulation, we have no way to understand what are the values and requirements behind those systems. Moreover, as collective responsibility is perceived to be eroding in many societies, alignment between social and individual values becomes less clear, and each one's notions of what is legally allowed, socially accepted and morally acceptable are no longer shared to the same extent.

Human dignity

As AI systems increasingly replace human decision-making, the risk is that we will become dependent on these systems. The margin between enhancement of capabilities and dependency on technology is narrow. More importantly, how autonomous and self-determining are we when AI systems determine the information we receive, and nudge us to choose healthy choices, to watch certain programs, to vote for given candidates? And how can we justify our own autonomous choices, when those are contrary to the ones our 'know-better' systems propose to us?

Due to their ability to mine data and make decisions, and powered by various abilities to interact with users, AI systems can potentially interfere with users, even if the aim is to contribute to their own good, thus exposing them to a form of paternalism. In a recent report by the AI4People work group, we described the main risks of AI. These have to do with the nature of being human and the human right to self-determination and autonomy, and include the danger of devaluing human skills, removing human responsibility, and reducing human control [56].

Moreover, by interpreting earlier choice behaviour as well as by inspecting users' goals and wishes, AI systems can potentially create preference profiles that are very reliable and that reflect their user's long-term agendas better than the less informed, more context-dependent and more temporarily distorted decisions of users themselves. This raises the issue of whether and in what circumstances such information should guide interactions with users, potentially even when users object to such interaction.

Ensuring human self-determination will impact the way assistive AI systems are designed: to what extent and in what circumstances is it morally justified to act towards another, potentially in freedom-restricting ways, when such action is not a response to that person's request, or is without her consent, or even against her expressed will? Assistive technology that is supposed to assist its user but that does so in ways that the user has not requested or not consented to is arguably ignoring the user's self-determination.

7.2.4 AI for Good

Beyond the risks that AI may pose, AI's impact will be defined by its contribution to human well-being and eco-social sustainability. The idea of AI for Good refers to this vision. Contribution to the achievement of UN Sustainable Development Goals is a main driver of AI for Good initiatives.

AI for Good projects also aim at extending access to AI, in particular to those regions and demographic groups less likely to have easy access to technology. Initiatives targeting developing countries, minorities and people with disabilities are examples of such projects. Other areas of AI for Good efforts are the use of AI technology to solve environmental questions, to support sustainable agriculture, and to promote low-carbon business practices. AI can also be used to help farmers, improve diagnostics, personalise learning or help refugees find jobs.

Nevertheless, and despite many events promoting AI for Good and an increasing number of organisations dedicated to the topic, most of these initiatives are small-scale and prototypical. A possible way forward is through incentives and nudges to bring large corporations to commit part of their work towards 'for Good' projects.

7.3 Super-intelligence

This book cannot end without a reflection on the issue of super-intelligence: the hypothetical capability of machines to surpass the brightest and most-gifted human minds. This relates to the quest to develop machines that not only reproduce but exceed human intelligence, or what is sometimes referred to as 'true AI'. It would suffice here to quote Luciano Floridi and state that *"True AI is not logically impossible, but it is utterly implausible"* [54], but actually I am not so sure about the logical possibility of such systems.

Humankind has always been engaged in developing super-scaled versions of itself. Airplanes can fly better than we can, cars, or even bicycles can move faster than we do, calculators can calculate square roots better than we can. All are superhuman from a specific perspective. However, as attributed to Edsger W. Dijkstra: "the question of whether a computer can think is no more interesting than the question of whether a submarine can swim."

Rather than focusing on the possibility, or not, of building super-intelligent machines, it is probably more relevant to discuss how we feel about it, and, from a responsibility/ethical perspective: should we do it, and what does it mean if we succeed? In the following, I will describe my views about all these issues.

Firstly, how do we feel about super-intelligent artefacts? Even before we think about whether it is possible and whether we should want to build such artefacts if it is possible, already our feelings about this are different from those we experience about other superhuman artefacts. What is it that makes intelligence different from flying or moving? We have no problem recognising that when we talk of an airplane flying, we mean a very different action than what birds do. That is, artificial flying is different from natural flying. In the same way, Artificial Intelligence is different from natural intelligence. It will, and in fact already does, complement us in many tasks, but it is a fundamentally different phenomenon than human intelligence.

We also tend to put intelligence and consciousness in the same box. What makes us conscious? Who and what are conscious entities? Newborn human babies? Monkeys? Chickens? Trees? Stones? What will make a machine conscious? As an illustration, consider the moment Lee Sedol was beaten by AlphaGo at the game of Go. Most newspapers showed a picture of the moment Lee realised he would lose: powerlessness, disbelief, sadness, all are expressions of his consciousness. Next to him was AlphaGo, a computer. It had no notion of what winning or losing meant, in fact it was not even aware it was playing a game. It was just following instructions and optimising some utility functions. Was it conscious?

Intelligence is not just about knowing, it is about feeling, enjoying, pushing limits. I often run marathons. I don't doubt that it is possible to build a 'running robot' but will it ever experience, and enjoy, what it means to run a marathon, to push through the pain and enjoy it?

On the issue of whether it is possible to build super-intelligent machines, the field is divided. Whereas many top scholars are sure of this possibility, the belief is not shared by all. One of the main supports for the possibility of super-intelligence is the so-called Church-Turing hypothesis [34].

Put simply, this thesis states that a mathematical function is computable if and only if it is computable by a Turing machine, i.e. by manipulation of symbols. This abstract machine can simulate what occurs in any computer, in a similar logical process. This being true, then there is a universal core to all computations which then means that any computation our brains can make can be simulated by a machine. The Church-Turing thesis thus argues that human intelligence can be reproduced by machine, but not that super-intelligence can be so achieved. Till date, we do not have a model more powerful than Turing Machine which can solve problems that Turing Machine cannot. However, it is not proved that a human brain can be represented as a Turing machine.

However, a Turing machine assumes infinite time and resources are available for the computation. Moreover, the (energetic) cost of such computations in an *in silico* machine are probably too large to allow practical development of such systems using the hardware we have available, nor or in the foreseeable future.

Another objection to super-intelligence is its conception of natural intelligence as a literal, single-dimension, linear graph of increasing amplitude, as it is portrayed by Nick Bostrom in his book *Superintelligence* [20]. However, intelligence is not one-dimensional. It is a complex of many types and modes of cognition, each one a continuum. Therefore, the paradigm of super-intelligence may fail in its assumption that if we manage to make machines intelligent in many different areas, it will entail super-intelligence in general. That is, intelligence is not compositional. Another way of putting it is not about finite vs infinite, but limits. For example, if I jump out of a plane I will reach terminal velocity due to friction. Are there similar frictions acting on intelligence? In his book *"Machines that Think"*, Toby Walsh discusses many more arguments against super-intelligence [133].

Moreover, super-intelligence rests on the assumption that intelligence is infinite. However, there is no other physical dimension in the universe that is infinite, as far as science knows so far. Temperature, space, time, speed are all finite. Only the abstract concept of numbers is infinite. It stands to reason that intelligence would itself also be finite.

Finally, there is the issue of whether we should want to build super-intelligence. Sure. As long as we build it to extend our capabilities to ensure human flourishing and well-being in a sustainable world, it is like extending our other capabilities to a super version of our selves. A main fear about super-intelligence is that those super-intelligent machines would rule out humans. However, remember, they are artefacts that we have built. The reason we need to build AI responsibly is exactly to ensure that the purpose we put into the machines, is the purpose we really need [103]. The goals that an AI system has can always be related to some human actor (that is why humans are the responsible agents). Besides, whatever goals the system has, they don't 'matter' to the system; its goals are not linked to any ulterior 'needs' of the system, they are given to it. So, in the words of Margaret Boden, the machine has no interest in ruling humankind. It will not take over because it couldn't care less [15].

Moreover, it is important to remember that true intelligence is not about 'winning'. It is about social skills, about collaboration and contribution to a greater good, about joining forces in order to survive and prosper. There is no reason to expect super-intelligence will be different.

On the other hand, we can also state that actually super-intelligence is easy. It is already here. It is the combined intelligence of all humans and other reasoning entities put together to work towards a common goal.

Or we can ask, does it matter? The ultimate goal of technology is to improve the human condition in a sustainable way for all of us and for our environment. As long as the motives are pure and we are achieving this goal, we are obliged to do so. This actually combines the different philosophical views on ethics, and brings us back to Chapter 3.

7.4 Responsible Artificial Intelligence

Responsible AI means that AI systems should be designed and implemented in ways that recognise and are sensitive to human interaction contexts without infringing on core values and human rights. Even though AI in itself does not absolve individuals from responsibility for their actions and decisions, the increasing complexity of AI systems renders attribution of responsibilities more difficult. Therefore, methods are needed that clarify responsibilities and make explicit what are the design choices, data and knowledge provenance, process and stakeholders.

Responsible AI means that AI systems must be understood as part of complex socio-technical systems. As such, an empirical/experimental ethics approach that can shape responsible (or good) AI, not only from the outside but also from within AI practices, is needed.

Responsible AI means that design, development and use of AI must take into account societal values and moral and ethical considerations, weigh the respective priorities of values held by different stakeholders in different multicultural contexts, explain its reasoning and guarantee transparency.

Responsible AI is more than the ticking of some ethical 'boxes' in a report, or the development of some add-on features, or switch-off buttons in AI systems. Rather, responsibility is fundamental to autonomy and one of the core stances underlying AI research and development.

But above all,

> **Responsible Artificial Intelligence is about human responsibility for the development of intelligent systems along fundamental human principles and values, to ensure human flourishing and well-being in a sustainable world.**

I look forward to a future when all AI is Responsible AI.

7.5 Further Reading

This book presents my views about the impact of AI. My aim was not to present a vision of the future, but to describe the current developments and the opportunities and challenges we face in ensuring that AI's impact will be a positive one for human well-being. In the last few years, several authors have proposed some interesting, in some cases profound, views of the future. You may want to check these:

- TEGMARK, M. *Life 3.0: Being Human in the Age of Artificial Intelligence.* Knopf, 2017

- HARARI, Y. N. *Homo Deus: A Brief History of Tomorrow.* Random House, 2016
- WALSH, T. *Machines that Think: The Future of Artificial Intelligence.* Prometheus Books, 2018

References

1. Open Letter to the European Commission Artificial Intelligence and Robotics. https://g8fip1kplyr33r3krz5b97d1-wpengine.netdna-ssl.com/wp-content/uploads/2018/04/RoboticsOpenLetter.pdf, 2017.
2. ADAM, C., CAVEDON, L., AND PADGHAM, L. "Hello Emily, how are you today?": Personalised dialogue in a toy to engage children. In *Proceedings of the 2010 Workshop on Companionable Dialogue Systems* (2010), CDS '10, Association for Computational Linguistics, pp. 19–24.
3. ALDEWERELD, H., ÁLVAREZ-NAPAGAO, S., DIGNUM, F., AND VÁZQUEZ-SALCEDA, J. Making norms concrete. In *9th International Conference on Autonomous Agents and Multiagent Systems (AAMAS 2010)* (2010), International Foundation for Autonomous Agents and Multiagent Systems, pp. 807–814.
4. ALDEWERELD, H., BOISSIER, O., DIGNUM, V., NORIEGA, P., PADGET, J. A., ET AL., Eds. *Social Coordination Frameworks for Social Technical Systems.* Springer, 2016.
5. ALDEWERELD, H., DIGNUM, V., AND TAN, Y. H. Design for values in software development. In *Handbook of Ethics, Values, and Technological Design: Sources, Theory, Values and Application Domains*, J. van den Hoven, P. E. Vermaas, and I. van de Poel, Eds. Springer Netherlands, 2014, pp. 831–845.
6. ALLEN, C., SMIT, I., AND WALLACH, W. Artificial morality: Top-down, bottom-up, and hybrid approaches. *Ethics and Information Technology 7*, 3 (2005), 149–155.
7. ANDERSON, M., ANDERSON, S. L., AND ARMEN, C. Towards machine ethics. In *AAAI-04 Workshop on Agent Organizations: Theory and Practice*, pp. 53–59.
8. ARMSTRONG, S., SANDBERG, A., AND BOSTROM, N. Thinking inside the box: Controlling and using an oracle AI. *Minds and Machines 22*, 4 (2012), 299–324.
9. ARNOLD, T., AND SCHEUTZ, M. The "big red button" is too late: an alternative model for the ethical evaluation of AI systems. *Ethics and Information Technology 20*, 1 (Mar 2018), 59–69.
10. AWAD, E., DSOUZA, S., KIM, R., SCHULZ, J., HENRICH, J., SHARIFF, A., BONNEFON, J., AND RAHWAN, I. The Moral Machine experiment. *Nature 563* (2018), 59–64.
11. BARKER, C. *Cultural Studies: Theory and Practice.* Sage, 2003.
12. BERREBY, F., BOURGNE, G., AND GABRIEL GANASCIA, J. Event-based and scenario-based causality for computational ethics. In *Proceedings of the 17th International Conference on Autonomous Agents and MultiAgent Systems, AAMAS* (2018), International Foundation for Autonomous Agents and Multiagent Systems, pp. 147–155.
13. BINMORE, K. *Natural justice.* Oxford University Press, 2005.
14. BJÖRKLUND, F. Differences in the justification of choices in moral dilemmas: Effects of gender, time pressure and dilemma seriousness. *Scandinavian Journal of Psychology 44*, 5 (2003), 459–466.

V. Dignum, *Responsible Artificial Intelligence*, Artificial Intelligence: Foundations, Theory, and Algorithms, https://doi.org/10.1007/978-3-030-30371-6

15. BODEN, M. Robot says: Whatever. *Aeon Essays,* https://aeon.co/essays/the-robots-wont-take-over-because-they-couldnt-care-less (2018).

16. BODEN, M., BRYSON, J., CALDWELL, D., DAUTENHAHN, K., EDWARDS, L., KEMBER, S., NEWMAN, P., PARRY, V., PEGMAN, G., RODDEN, T., ET AL. Principles of robotics: regulating robots in the real world. *Connection Science* **29**, 2 (2017), 124–129.

17. BONNEFON, J.-F., SHARIFF, A., AND RAHWAN, I. The social dilemma of autonomous vehicles. *Science* **352**, 6293 (2016), 1573–1576.

18. BONNEMAINS, V., SAUREL, C., AND TESSIER, C. Embedded ethics: some technical and ethical challenges. *Ethics and Information Technology* **20**, 1 (Mar 2018), 41–58.

19. BORDINI, R. H., HÜBNER, J. F., AND WOOLDRIDGE, M. *Programming Multi-Agent Systems in AgentSpeak Using Jason.* John Wiley & Sons, 2007.

20. BOSTROM, N. *Superintelligence: Paths, Dangers, Strategies.* Oxford University Press, 2014.

21. BOSTROM, N., AND YUDKOWSKY, E. The ethics of artificial intelligence. *The Cambridge Handbook of Artificial Intelligence* (2014), 316–334.

22. BRADSHAW, J. M., DIGNUM, V., JONKER, C., AND SIERHUIS, M. Human-agent-robot teamwork. *IEEE Intelligent Systems* **27**, 2 (2012), 8–13.

23. BRATMAN, M. E. *Intentions, Plans, and Practical Reason.* CSLI, 1987.

24. BRUNDAGE, M., AVIN, S., CLARK, J., TONER, H., ECKERSLEY, P., GARFINKEL, B., DAFOE, A., SCHARRE, P., ZEITZOFF, T., FILAR, B., ET AL. The malicious use of artificial intelligence: Forecasting, prevention, and mitigation. *arXiv preprint arXiv:1802.07228* (2018).

25. BRYSON, J., AND WINFIELD, A. Standardizing ethical design for artificial intelligence and autonomous systems. *Computer* **50**, 5 (May 2017), 116–119.

26. BRYSON, J. J. Patiency is not a virtue: the design of intelligent systems and systems of ethics. *Ethics and Information Technology* **20**, 1 (Mar 2018), 15–26.

27. CASTELFRANCHI, C. Guarantees for autonomy in cognitive agent architecture. In *Intelligent Agents* (1995), M. J. Wooldridge and N. R. Jennings, Eds., vol. **890** of *Lecture Notes in Computer Science*, Springer, pp. 56–70.

28. CAVAZZA, M., SMITH, C., CHARLTON, D., CROOK, N., BOYE, J., PULMAN, S., MOILA-NEN, K., PIZZI, D., DE LA CAMARA, R. S., AND TURUNEN, M. Persuasive dialogue based on a narrative theory: An ECA implementation. In *Persuasive Technology, Proceedings of the 5th International Conference on Persuasive Technology (PERSUASIVE'10)* (2010), vol. **6137** of *Lecture Notes in Computer Science*, Springer-Verlag, pp. 250–261.

29. COINTE, N., BONNET, G., AND BOISSIER, O. Ethical judgment of agents' behaviors in multi-agent systems. In *Proceedings of the 2016 International Conference on Autonomous Agents and Multiagent Systems (AAMAS 2016)* (2016), International Foundation for Autonomous Agents and Multiagent Systems, pp. 1106–1114.

30. CONITZER, V., SINNOTT-ARMSTRONG, W., BORG, J. S., DENG, Y., AND KRAMER, M. Moral decision making frameworks for artificial intelligence. In *Proceedings of the Twenty-Sixth International Joint Conference on Artificial Intelligence (IJCAI 2017)* (2017), pp. 4831–4835.

31. CRANEFIELD, S., WINIKOFF, M., DIGNUM, V., AND DIGNUM, F. No pizza for you: Value-based plan selection in BDI agents. In *Proceedings of the Twenty-Sixth International Joint Conference on Artificial Intelligence (IJCAI 2017)* (2017), pp. 1–16.

32. DAHL, R. *Democracy and its Critics.* Yale University Press, 1989.

33. DASTANI, M. 2APL: a practical agent programming language. *Autonomous Agents and Multi-Agent Systems* **16**, 3 (Jun 2008), 214–248.

34. DAVIS, M. *The Undecidable: Basic Papers on Undecidable Propositions, Unsolvable Problems, and Computable Functions.* Dover, 1965.

35. DENIS, L., Ed. *Kant: The Metaphysics of Morals.* Cambridge University Press, 2017.

36. DENNETT, D. C. *Freedom Evolves.* Viking, 2003.

37. DENNIS, L. A., FISHER, M., AND WINFIELD, A. Towards verifiably ethical robot behaviour. In *Workshops at the Twenty-Ninth AAAI Conference on Artificial Intelligence* (2015).

38. DIAS, J., MASCARENHAS, S., AND PAIVA, A. FAtiMA Modular: Towards an agent architecture with a generic appraisal framework. In *Emotion modeling*, T. Bosse, J. Broekens, J. Dias, and J. van der Zwaan, Eds., vol. *8750* of *Lecture Notes in Computer Science*. Springer, 2014, pp. 44–56.

39. DIGNUM, V. *A model for organizational interaction: based on agents, founded in logic*. SIKS, 2004.

40. DIGNUM, V. Responsible autonomy. In *Proceedings of the Twenty-Sixth International Joint Conference on Artificial Intelligence (IJCAI 2017)* (2017), pp. 4698–4704.

41. DIGNUM, V. Ethics in artificial intelligence: introduction to the special issue. *Ethics and Information Technology* **20**, 1 (Mar 2018), 1–3.

42. DIGNUM, V., BALDONI, M., BAROGLIO, C., CAON, M., CHATILA, R., DENNIS, L., GENOVA, G., KLIESS, M., LOPEZ-SANCHEZ, M., MICALIZIO, R., PAVON, J., SLAVKOVIK, M., SMAKMAN, M., VAN STEENBERGEN, M., TEDESCHI, S., VAN DER TORRE, L., VILLATA, S., DE WILDT, T., AND HAIM, G. Ethics by design: necessity or curse? In *Proceedings of the 1st International Conference on AI Ethics and Society* (2018), ACM, pp. 60–66.

43. DOMINGOS, P. *The Master Algorithm: How the Quest for the Ultimate Learning Machine Will Remake Our World*. Basic Books, 2015.

44. DOYLE, J. The foundations of psychology: A logico-computational inquiry into the concept of mind. In *Philosophy and AI: Essays at the Interface*, R. Cummins and J. Pollock, Eds. MIT Press, 1991, pp. 39–77.

45. DREYFUS, H., DREYFUS, S. E., AND ATHANASIOU, T. *Mind over machine*. Simon and Schuster, 2000.

46. DRYZEK, J. S., AND LIST, C. Social choice theory and deliberative democracy: a reconciliation. *British Journal of Political Science 33*, 1 (2003), 1–28.

47. DWORK, C., HARDT, M., PITASSI, T., REINGOLD, O., AND ZEMEL, R. S. Fairness through awareness. In *Innovations in Theoretical Computer Science 2012* (2012), ACM, pp. 214–226.

48. EISENHARDT, K. M. Agency theory: An assessment and review. *The Academy of Management Review* **14**, 1 (1989), 57–74.

49. ETZIONI, O. No, the experts don't think superintelligent AI is a threat to humanity. *MIT Technology Review* (2016).

50. EUROPEAN PARLIAMENT. Motion for a European Parliament Resolution, with recommendations to the Commission on Civil Law Rules on Robotics. `http://www.europarl.europa.eu/doceo/document/A-8-2017-0005_EN.html?redirect`, 2017.

51. FISHKIN, J. S. *When the People Speak: Deliberative Democracy and Public Consultation*. Oxford University Press, 2011.

52. FITTS, P. M. Human engineering for an effective air-navigation and traffic-control system. *National Research Council, Committee on Aviation Psychology* (1951).

53. FLORIDI, L. *The ethics of information*. Oxford University Press, 2013.

54. FLORIDI, L. Should we be afraid of AI? *Aeon Essays,* `https://aeon.co/essays/true-ai-is-both-logically-possible-and-utterly-implausible` (2016).

55. FLORIDI, L. Soft ethics and the governance of the digital. *Philosophy & Technology 31*, 1 (Mar 2018), 1–8.

56. FLORIDI, L., COWLS, J., BELTRAMETTI, M., CHATILA, R., CHAZERAND, P., DIGNUM, V., LUETGE, C., MADELIN, R., PAGALLO, U., ROSSI, F., SCHAFER, B., VALCKE, P., AND VAYENA, E. AI4People - an ethical framework for a good AI society: Opportunities, risks, principles, and recommendations. *Minds and Machines* **28**, 4 (2018), 687–707.

57. FLORIDI, L., AND SANDERS, J. On the morality of artificial agents. *Minds and Machines* **14**, 3 (2004), 349–379.

58. FOOT, P. The problem of abortion and the doctrine of double effect. *Oxford Review* **5** (1967), 5–15.

59. FRANK, M. R., SUN, L., CEBRIAN, M., YOUN, H., AND RAHWAN, I. Small cities face greater impact from automation. *Journal of The Royal Society Interface* **15**, 139 (2018).

60. FRIEDMAN, B., KAHN, P. H., AND BORNING, A. Value sensitive design and information systems. *Advances in Management Information Systems* **6** (2006), 348–372.

61. GARDNER, H. *Frames of Mind: The Theory of Multiple Intelligences*. Basic Books, 2011.

62. GAVRILETS, S., AND VOSE, A. The dynamics of Machiavellian intelligence. *Proceedings of the National Academy of Sciences* **103**, 45 (2006), 16823–16828.

63. GIGERENZER, G. Moral satisficing: Rethinking moral behavior as bounded rationality. *Topics in Cognitive Science* **2**, 3 (2010), 528–554.

64. GOODRICH, M. A., AND SCHULTZ, A. C. Human-robot interaction: a survey. *Foundations and Trends in Human-Computer Interaction* **1**, 3 (2007), 203–275.

65. GOTTERBARN, D., BRUCKMAN, A., FLICK, C., MILLER, K., AND WOLF, M. J. ACM code of ethics: a guide for positive action. *Communications of the ACM* **61**, 1 (2018), 121–128.

66. GRAHAM, J., NOSEK, B., HAIDT, J., IYER, R., KOLEVA, S., AND DITTO, P. Mapping the moral domain. *Journal of Personality and Social Psychology* **101**, 2 (2011), 366–385.

67. GRICE, H. P. *Logic and conversation*. Academic Press, 1975.

68. GROSSI, D., MEYER, J.-J. CH., AND DIGNUM, F. Counts-As: Classification or constitution? An answer using modal logic. In *Deontic Logic and Artificial Normative Systems: Proceedings of the Eighth International Workshop on Deontic Logic in Computer Science (DEON'06)* (2006), L. Goble and J.-J. Ch. Meyer, Eds., vol. *4048* of *Lecture Notes in Artificial Intelligence*, Springer-Verlag.

69. GUNKEL, D. J. *Robot Rights*. MIT Press, 2018.

70. GUNNING, D. Explainable Artificial Intelligence (XAI). `https://www.darpa.mil/program/explainable-artificial-intelligence`, 2018.

71. HARARI, Y. N. *Homo Deus: A Brief History of Tomorrow*. Random House, 2016.

72. HELBING, D., FREY, B. S., GIGERENZER, G., HAFEN, E., HAGNER, M., HOFSTETTER, Y., VAN DEN HOVEN, J., ZICARI, R. V., AND ZWITTER, A. Will democracy survive big data and artificial intelligence? *Scientific American* `https://www.scientificamerican.com/article/will-democracy-survive-big-data-and-artificial-intelligence/` (2017).

73. HOFSTEDE, G. *Culture's Consequences: Comparing Values, Behaviors, Institutions and Organizations*. Sage, 2001.

74. JENNINGS, N. R. Agent-oriented software engineering. In *Multiple Approaches to Intelligent Systems* (1999), I. Imam, Y. Kodratoff, A. El-Dessouki, and M. Ali, Eds., Springer, pp. 4–10.

75. JENNINGS, N. R., AND WOOLDRIDGE, M. J. *Agent Technology: Foundations, Applications, and Markets*. Springer Science & Business Media, 1998.

76. JONES, A., AND SERGOT, M. On the characterization of law and computer systems. In *Deontic Logic in Computer Science: Normative System Specification* (1993), J.-J. Meyer and R. Wieringa, Eds., Wiley, pp. 275–307.

77. KIM, R., KLEIMAN-WEINER, M., ABELIUK, A., AWAD, E., DSOUZA, S., TENENBAUM, J., AND RAHWAN, I. A Computational Model of Commonsense Moral Decision Making. In *AAAI/ACM Conference on Artificial Intelligence, Ethics and Society (AIES)* (2018), ACM, pp. 197–203.

78. KLENK, M., MOLINEAUX, M., AND AHA, D. W. Goal-driven autonomy for responding to unexpected events in strategy simulations. *Computational Intelligence* **29**, 2 (2012), 187–206.

79. KUIPERS, B. How can we trust a robot? *Commun. ACM* **61**, 3 (Feb. 2018), 86–95.

80. KURZWEIL, R. *The Singularity is Near: When Humans Transcend Biology.* Penguin, 2005.

81. LANGLEY, P. The changing science of machine learning. *Machine Learning* **82**, 3 (Mar 2011), 275–279.

82. LE, Q. V., MONGA, R., DEVIN, M., CORRADO, G., CHEN, K., RANZATO, M., DEAN, J., AND NG, A. Y. Building high-level features using large scale unsupervised learning. *CoRR abs/1112.6209* (2011).

83. LECUN, Y., BENGIO, Y., AND HINTON, G. Deep learning. *Nature* **521**, 7553 (2015), 436–444.

84. LI, W., SADIGH, D., SASTRY, S., AND SESHIA, S. Synthesis for human-in-the-loop control systems. In *Tools and Algorithms for the Construction and Analysis of Systems: 20th International Conference, (TACAS 2014)*, E. Ábrahám and K. Havelund, Eds., vol. *8413* of *Lecture Notes in Computer Science.* Springer, 2014, pp. 470–484.

85. MALLE, B. F. Integrating robot ethics and machine morality: the study and design of moral competence in robots. *Ethics and Information Technology* **8**, 4 (2016), 243–256.

86. MALLE, B. F., SCHEUTZ, M., ARNOLD, T., VOIKLIS, J., AND CUSIMANO, C. Sacrifice one for the good of many?: People apply different moral norms to human and robot agents. In *Proceedings of the Tenth Annual ACM/IEEE International Conference on Human-Robot Interaction* (2015), HRI '15, ACM, pp. 117–124.

87. MCCARTHY, J., MINSKY, M. L., ROCHESTER, N., AND SHANNON, C. E. A proposal for the Dartmouth summer research project on Artificial Intelligence, August 31, 1955. *AI Magazine* **27**, 4 (2006), 12–14.

88. MCDERMOTT, D. Artificial Intelligence and Consciousness. In *The Cambridge Handbook of Consciousness*, P. Zelazo, M. Moscovitch, and E. Thompson, Eds. 2007, pp. 117–150.

89. MICELI, M., AND CASTELFRANCHI, C. A cognitive approach to values. *Journal for the Theory of Social Behaviour* **19**, 2 (1989), 169–193. doi: 10.1111/j.1468-5914.1989.tb00143.x.

90. MICHALSKI, R. S., CARBONELL, J. G., AND MITCHELL, T. M. *Machine Learning: An Artificial Intelligence Approach.* Springer Science & Business Media, 1983.

91. MILL, J. *Utilitarianism.* Oxford University Press, 1998.

92. MILLER, T. Explanation in artificial intelligence: Insights from the social sciences. *Artificial Intelligence* **267** (2019), 1 – 38.

93. MISENER, J., AND SHLADOVER, S. Path investigations in vehicle-roadside cooperation and safety: A foundation for safety and vehicle-infrastructure integration research. In *Intelligent Transportation Systems Conference, 2006* (2006), IEEE, pp. 9–16.

94. MODGIL, S., AND PRAKKEN, H. A general account of argumentation with preferences. *Artificial Intelligence* **195** (2013), 361–397.

95. NASS, C., AND MOON, Y. Machines and mindlessness: Social responses to computers. *Journal of Social Issues* **56**, 1 (2002), 81–103.

96. NOOTHIGATTU, R., GAIKWAD, S. N. S., AWAD, E., DSOUZA, S., RAHWAN, I., RAVIKUMAR, P., AND PROCACCIA, A. D. A voting-based system for ethical decision making. *CoRR abs/1709.06692* (2017).

97. O'NEILL, C. *Weapons of Math Destruction: How Big Data Increases Inequality and Threatens Democracy.* Crown, 2016.

98. PEDRESCHI, D., RUGGIERI, S., AND TURINI, F. Discrimination-aware data mining. In *Proceedings of the 14th ACM SIGKDD International Conference on Knowledge Discovery and Data Mining* (2008), pp. 560–568.

99. PICARD, R. W. Affective Computing: Challenges. *International Journal of Human-Computer Studies* **59**, 1-2 (2003), 55–64.

100. RAHWAN, I. Society-in-the-loop: programming the algorithmic social contract. *Ethics and Information Technology* **20**, 1 (Mar 2018), 5–14.

101. ROKEACH, M. Rokeach Values Survey. In *The Nature of Human Values*, M. Rokeach, Ed. The Free Press, 1973.

102. ROYAKKERS, L., AND ORBONS, S. Design for Values in the armed forces: nonlethal weapons and military robots. In *Handbook of Ethics, Values, and Technological Design: Sources, Theory, Values and Application Domains*, J. van den Hoven, P. E. Vermaas, and I. van de Poel, Eds. Springer, 2015, pp. 613–638.

103. RUSSELL, S. Should we fear supersmart robots? *Scientific American 314*, 6 (2016), 58–59.

104. RUSSELL, S., AND NORVIG, P. *Artificial Intelligence: A Modern Approach*, 3rd ed. Pearson Education, 2009.

105. RUTTKAY, Z., AND PELACHAUD, C., Eds. *From Brows to Trust: Evaluating Embodied Conversational Agents*. Springer Science & Business Media, 2004.

106. SCHOFIELD, P., Ed. *The Collected Works of Jeremy Bentham: An Introduction to the Principles of Morals and Legislation*. Clarendon Press, 1996.

107. SCHWARTZ, S. A theory of cultural value orientations: Explication and applications. *Comparative sociology 5*, 2 (2006), 137–182.

108. SCHWARTZ, S. An overview of the Schwartz theory of basic values. *Online Readings in Psychology and Culture 2*, 1 (2012). doi: 10.9707/2307-0919.1116.

109. SEARLE, J. *The Construction of Social Reality*. Simon and Schuster, 1995.

110. SEARLE, J. R. Minds, brains, and programs. *Behavioral and Brain Sciences 3*, 3 (1980), 417–424.

111. SERRAMIA, M., LOPEZ-SANCHEZ, M., RODRIGUEZ-AGUILAR, J. A., RODRIGUEZ, M., WOOLDRIDGE, M., MORALES, J., AND ANSOTEGUI, C. Moral values in norm decision making. In *Proceedings of the 17th International Conference on Autonomous Agents and MultiAgent Systems (AAMAS 2018)* (2018), International Foundation for Autonomous Agents and Multiagent Systems, pp. 1294–1302.

112. SHARKEY, A. Can robots be responsible moral agents? And why should we care? *Connection Science 29*, 3 (2017), 210–216.

113. SHAW, N. P., STÖCKEL, A., ORR, R. W., LIDBETTER, T. F., AND COHEN, R. Towards provably moral AI agents in bottom-up learning frameworks. In *2018 AAAI Spring Symposium Series* (2018), pp. 69–75.

114. SINNOTT-ARMSTRONG, W. *Moral Dilemmas*. Wiley Online Library, 1988.

115. STERNBERG, R. J. A model for ethical reasoning. *Review of General Psychology 16*, 4 (2012), 319–326.

116. STONE, P., BROOKS, R., BRYNJOLFSSON, E., CALO, R., ETZIONI, O., HAGER, G., HIRSCHBERG, J., KALYANAKRISHNAN, S., KAMAR, E., KRAUS, S., LEYTON-BROWN, K., PARKES, D., PRESS, W., SAXENIAN, A., SHAH, J., TAMBE, M., AND TELLER, A. Artificial Intelligence and Life in 2030: One Hundred Year Study on Artificial Intelligence: Report of the 2015-2016 Study Panel. https://ai100.stanford.edu/2016-report, 2016.

117. TADDEO, M. The limits of deterrence theory in cyberspace. *Philosophy & Technology 31*, 3 (2018), 339–355.

118. TEGMARK, M. *Life 3.0: Being Human in the Age of Artificial Intelligence*. Knopf, 2017.

119. TREWAVAS, A. Green plants as intelligent organisms. *Trends in Plant Science 10*, 9 (2005), 413 – 419.

120. TURING, A. Computing machinery and intelligence. *Mind 59*, 236 (1950), 433–460.

121. VAMPLEW, P., DAZELEY, R., FOALE, C., FIRMIN, S., AND MUMMERY, J. Human-aligned artificial intelligence is a multiobjective problem. *Ethics and Information Technology 20*, 1 (Mar 2018), 27–40.

122. VAN DE POEL, I. Translating values into design requirements. In *Philosophy and Engineering: Reflections on Practice, Principles and Process*, D. Michelfelder, N. McCarthy, and D. Goldberg, Eds. Springer Netherlands, 2013, pp. 253–266.

123. VAN DE POEL, I. An ethical framework for evaluating experimental technology. *Science and Engineering Ethics 22*, 3 (Jun 2016), 667–686.

124. VAN DEN HOVEN, J. Design for values and values for design. *Information Age, Journal of the Australian Computer Society 7*, 2 (2005), 4–7.

125. VAN DEN HOVEN, J. ICT and value sensitive design. In *The Information Society: Innovation, Legitimacy, Ethics and Democracy. In honor of Professor Jacques Berleur S.J.*, P. Goujon, S. Lavelle, P. Duquenoy, K. Kimppa, and V. Laurent, Eds., vol. 233 of *IFIP International Federation for Information Processing*. Springer, 2007, pp. 67–72.

126. VAN WYNSBERGHE, A., AND ROBBINS, S. Critiquing the reasons for making artificial moral agents. *Science and Engineering Ethics* (2018), 1–17.

127. VÁZQUEZ-SALCEDA, J., ALDEWERELD, H., GROSSI, D., AND DIGNUM, F. From human regulations to regulated software agents' behaviour. *Journal of Artificial Intelligence and Law* **16** (2008), 73–87.

128. VERDIESEN, I., DIGNUM, V., AND VAN DEN HOVEN, J. Measuring moral acceptability in e-deliberation: A practical application of ethics by participation. *ACM Transactions on Internet Technology (TOIT)* **18**, 4 (2018), 43.

129. VERUGGIO, G., AND OPERTO, F. Roboethics: A bottom-up interdisciplinary discourse in the field of applied ethics in robotics. *International Review of Information Ethics* **6**, 12 (2006), 2–8.

130. VINGE, V. Technological singularity. In *VISION-21 Symposium sponsored by NASA Lewis Research Center and the Ohio Aerospace Institute* (1993), pp. 30–31.

131. VON SCHOMBERG, R. A vision of responsible innovation. In *Responsible Innovation*, R. Owen, M. Heintz, and J. Bessant, Eds. John Wiley, 2013, pp. 51–74.

132. WALLACH, W., AND ALLEN, C. *Moral Machines: Teaching Robots Right from Wrong*. Oxford University Press, 2008.

133. WALSH, T. *Machines that Think: The Future of Artificial Intelligence*. Prometheus Books, 2018.

134. WINIKOFF, M. Towards Trusting Autonomous Systems. In *Fifth Workshop on Engineering Multi-Agent Systems (EMAS)* (2017).

135. WINIKOFF, M., DIGNUM, V., AND DIGNUM, F. Why bad coffee? Explaining agent plans with valuings. In *International Conference on Computer Safety, Reliability, and Security* (2018), B. Gallina, A. Skavhaug, E. Schoitsch, and F. Bitsch, Eds., vol. 11094 of *Lecture Notes in Computer Science*, Springer, pp. 521–534.

136. WOOLDRIDGE, M. *An Introduction to Multiagent Systems*. John Wiley & Sons, 2009.

137. WOOLDRIDGE, M., AND JENNINGS, N. R. Intelligent agents: theory and practice. *The Knowledge Engineering Review* **10**, 2 (1995), 115–152.

Printed in the United States
By Bookmasters